16.50

P9-DDO-941

Food and beverage management

Food and beverage management

DAVID A. FEARN

LONDON BUTTERWORTHS

THE BUTTERWORTH GROUP

ENGLAND
Butterworth & Co (Publishers) Ltd
London: 88 Kingsway, WC2B 6AB

AUSTRALIA
Butterworths Pty Ltd
Sydney: 586 Pacific Highway, NSW 2067
Melbourne: 343 Little Collins Street, 3000
Brisbane: 240 Queen Street, 4000

CANADA
Butterworth & Co (Canada) Ltd
Toronto: 14 Curity Avenue, 374

NEW ZEALAND
Butterworths of New Zealand Ltd
Wellington: 26-28 Waring Taylor Street, 1

SOUTH AFRICA
Butterworth & Co (South Africa) (Pty) Ltd
Durban: 152-154 Gale Street

First published 1973

© D. A. FEARN, 1973

ISBN 0 408 70158 7

Printed in Great Britain by
Redwood Press Limited
Trowbridge, Wiltshire

and bound by James Burn Ltd
Esher, Surrey

Preface

My objective in producing this book is to provide the hotel and catering industry with a comprehensive reference to the complexities of managing food and beverage operations.

The purpose underlying this objective is to fill the serious void which exists in the industry's bookshelves, and I believe that management and students in the industry will find useful the fact that the subjects included in the book are obtainable between one set of covers.

The need for a volume of this kind makes itself apparent every day in my work; and in attempting to cater for everyone I have concentrated upon the use of simple straightforward language and diagrams, so that it might be helpful to the smallest grill bar operator as well as the most luxurious hotel or restaurant.

One thing that I have tried to do is to show how management techniques and thinking may be *profitably* used in food and beverage operations, and should only one caterer feel rewarded after reading and utilising some of the techniques contained within, my late nights and early mornings will have been worth while.

Finally, it should be mentioned that the book was produced during an extremely inflationary period, and certain data such as food and beverage prices and wages, current when the original research was done, are now no longer up to date. Nevertheless, the basic accounting systems, recommendations, etc., which are given are still applicable.

David A. Fearn

Contents

1

Food and beverage management—its meaning

The term food and beverage management originated in the USA, where the very size of hotel operations demanded management specialisation in order that they could function adequately. Subsequently, smaller hotels in the UK and elsewhere found that their operations demanded a higher degree of specialisation than they had hitherto recognised. The conventional management structure of hotels did not allow the management team to communicate easily, or to isolate and achieve financial and management objectives.

DEPARTMENTALISATION

By considering the departmental structure of hotels, management arrived at a rational basis on which to apportion income and costs to particular members of the management team. This had been almost impossible to do previously.

Consider the organisation structure shown in *Figure 1.1*, where income and costs have been assigned as far as possible. In some cases departmental heads have been made responsible for labour costs within their departments. However, this is comparatively rare.

The influence of the organisation on management performance is to inhibit it, by simply allowing the general manager to administer every department personally. In some cases, one man will have up to ten or fifteen departmental heads, and three or four hundred staff reporting directly to him. It is obvious that even the most remarkable managers cannot adequately undertake this huge task of delegation.

Some hotels are too small to adopt any but the type of organisation shown and management will probably consist of one manager and assistant, or just one manager. In cases like this, management

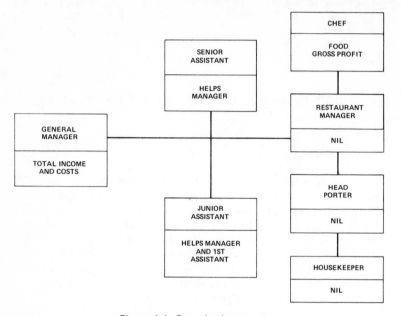

Figure 1.1. Organisation structure

will have specific responsibilities which will not overlap. Any division is acceptable provided that it is traceable to objectives which may be measured in practical terms.

EXAMPLE: BLUE BAY HOTEL

Two brothers operating a small hotel found that they could manage it adequately by carefully subdividing the hotel's activities between them. Each covered the other's off-duty periods but did not assume responsibility for the other's function.

Their first consideration was to divide what they considered the most important functions, which were sales and marketing, administration and accounting. The hotel's departments were then divided between them according to the time allowed them by the main function, as shown in *Table 1.1*.

By using a well-constructed accountancy presentation the brothers were able to monitor their performance by allotting personal responsibilities to each department. It was comparatively easy to transfer responsibilities when they expanded their activities by selecting a manager and assistant to take over food and beverage and rooms, respectively.

Responsibility accounting

In larger hotels departmentalisation becomes simpler. By subdividing departmental responsibilities the structural and financial objectives shown in *Figure 1.2* may be established. This structure allows each manager and departmental head to work for objectives which, when achieved, will result in a net profit for the whole unit.

The whole is monitored by accounts presentations, constructed to show the performance of management in attaining their prescribed

Table 1.1 Division of functions

Main function	Brother A Accounting	Brother B Sales
	Restaurant Kitchen	Rooms Bar

objectives. Accountancy presentations of this nature are termed 'responsibility accounting'. An example of a responsibility accounting presentation is shown in *Figure 1.3*, pages 6 and 7, together with a comprehensive hotel organisation structure (*Figure 1.4*, page 8).

It is of no consequence what areas of specialisation are adopted as long as they comply with the following conditions:

(a) The departments administered by each manager must be related, e.g. kitchen and restaurant.

(b) The management performance of each manager or departmental head must be adequately monitored by responsibility accounts.

SUPERVISION OF STAFF

The responsibilities of the food and beverage manager are concerned with the following departments: kitchen, bars, restaurants, cellar, floor service, lounge service, stillroom, glass and pot wash, and stores (food).

Owing to the nature of hotels, these departments tend to be the most complex of all hotel departments, and, therefore, the food and beverage manager, apart from having obvious technical skills, must be able to delegate adequately and organise rationally.

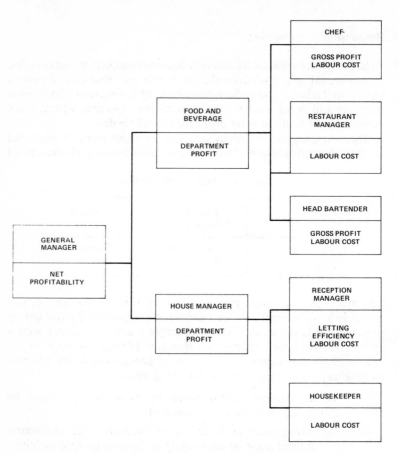

Figure 1.2. Structural and financial objectives

The supervisory responsibilities are to see that the requirements, in terms of the establishment's standards of work, are carried out in the various departments under him. A major part of this is to ensure that departmental heads know precisely what is expected of them, and that they in turn know what is expected of their staff. One of the most logical ways to do this is to isolate the key result areas of each grade of staff through detailed job specifications, as shown in *Table 1.2*. From these areas, objectives (both financial and creative) may be established and the purpose beyond the objective made known to staff to assist understanding and team work.

By creating objectives, success criteria have been built into the tasks set, and it is the function of management to supervise through the performance of staff against their objectives.

Table 1.2 Job specification—cellarman

Tasks	Objectives	Purpose
To maintain stock at prescribed levels	To turn stock round nine to ten times per annum	To reduce working capital commitment
To keep cellar clean and tidy	To preserve condition of stock held in cellar	Reduction of ullages and administrative time wasted by returns
To ensure that stock is exchanged only for a bona fide check (requisition)	To ensure that all stock issued is requisitioned	Elimination of pilferage
To ensure that stock received is adequately documented	To ensure that stock paid for has been received	Elimination of short deliveries
To provide management with orders necessary to replenish to maximum stock levels	To ensure that orders are placed which are necessary to maintain stock levels	To allow the hotel to continually offer selected products to guests

Supervision is, of course, not only concerned with this, but with the social skills of management in dealing with personnel. Most managers are quite good at this, and it is the other fields of isolating objectives in which they experience problems.

Supervisory procedure

- (*a*) Draw up job specification.
- (*b*) Isolate objectives (key result areas) with member of staff.
- (*c*) Establish the purpose beyond the objective.
- (*d*) Explain the purpose to the member of staff.
- (*e*) Monitor the performance through personal inspection and accounts.
- (*f*) Take action if performance varies from objective and affects purpose.

Unit: The Golden Sands Hotel										Accounting period No.: 2	
Department	No.	Net sales £	%	Direct materials £	%	Gross margin £	%	Wages and staff costs £	%	Net margin £
Accommodation	1	1 228	100	13	1	1 215	100	274	22	941
Food	2	4 439	100	1 756	39	2 683	61	1 858	42	825
Liquor	2	2 629	100	1 315	50	1 314	50	227	8	1 087
Other operated depts.	3	34	100	24	70	10	30	—		10
Total		£8 330	100	£3 108	37	£5 222	63	£2 359	28	£2 863
Other income	4	81	100	—		81		—		81
Administration	5	8 411	100	3 108	36	5 303	64	2 359 489	29	2 944
Advertising	6									
Heat, light, power	7									
General	8									
Total	9			—		—		£489		—
Hotel control level	10	8 411	100	3 108	36	5 303	64	2 848	34	2 455
Rent, rates, insurance	11									
Other additions/deduc.	12									
Depreciation	13									
Repairs and maintenance	14									
Garden	15	—						295		
Total		—		—		—		£295		—
Net loss		£8 411	100	£3 108	36	£5 303	64	£3 143	40	£2 160

Figure 1.3. Hotel responsibility accounting presentation

From: 1 Feb. 1969   To: 28 Feb. 1969

bu- ts	%	Profit — Loss £	%	4-Week budget £	%	Actual cumu'tive £	%	Budget cumu'tive £	%	4-Week variance £	%
90	15	751	63	835	70	1 584	56	3 245	65	84	7
08	5	617	14	885	20	238	2	1 500	20	268	6
22	1	1 065	41	1 091	42	2 327	37	2 800	40	26	1
.		10	30	10	30	19	20	20	30	—	—
20	5	£2 443	30	£2 821	34	£4 168	21	£7 565	36	£378	4
.		81	—	81	—	205		205		—	—
20	5	2 524	30	2 902	34	4 373	22	7 770	37	378	4
23		612	7	420	5	1 750	8	1 364	6	192	2
64		64	1	84	1	220	1	220	2	(20)	—
11		511	6	336	4	768	4	1 050	5	175	2
18)		(318)	(4)	(318)	(4)	(566)	(2)	(630)	(3)	—	—
80		£869	10	£522	6	£2 172	11	£2 004	10	£347	4
00	10	1 655	20	2 380	28	2 201	11	5 670	27	725	8
96		96	1	96	1	288	1	288	1	—	—
21		521	6	521	6	1 456	7	1 456	7	—	—
18		318	4	318	4	954	5	954	5	—	—
88		588	7	588	7	1 407	7	1 407	7	—	—
95		390	5	300	4	1 043	5	500	3	90	1
18		£1 913	23	£1 823	22	£5 148	25	£4 605	23	£90	1
18	27	(£258)	(3)	£557	6	(£2 947)	(14)	£840	4	£815	9
		Loss		Profit		Loss		Profit		Unfavourable	

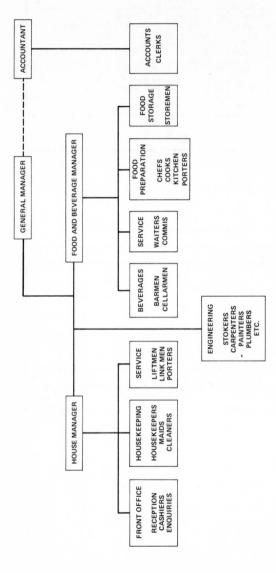

Figure 1.4. Hotel organisation structure

COMMUNICATION BETWEEN MANAGEMENT AND STAFF

More so than any of the other departments, the food and beverage departments require communications to be accurate and timely. Although adequate explanation of objectives and job purpose goes a long way towards achieving this, it must be acknowledged as a continuous process. Management must delegate carefully and explicitly through sufficient explanation, management meetings, and correct procedures.

Explicit explanation by management to staff may be considered in two sections: (*a*) repetitive procedures; (*b*) *ad hoc* procedures.

Repetitive procedures

These are procedures which involve everyday work, e.g. formulation of menu composition, bar close-down procedures. They must be correctly carried out daily or weekly. The only way management can ensure complete compliance with standard procedures is to make sure they are understood from the start. This may be done by providing induction courses, staff manuals, adequate initial instructions from departmental heads or management, or even teaching machine programmes.

Although these procedures are adopted by many companies for the reasons noted they are seldom maintained. The prime reason is that management does not realise that the procedures are going off-course until it is too late to prevent a problem occurring. Management cognisant of the possible breakdown of procedures will systematically observe the work of their departments so that any deviation is noticed immediately and corrected. This is termed 'management by exception'. It takes a little time to master, as it involves disciplining one's thinking and observation.

Ad hoc procedures

These are procedures which happen from time to time and could necessitate completely different arrangements on each occasion, e.g. functions or special conference arrangements. They do, however, require that *all* arrangements be communicated down the line to everyone concerned. This would appear to be fundamental. However, the lack of communication apparent in some establishments never ceases to amaze conference and course organisers, not the least banqueters and residential guests.

When one is dealing with special arrangements a pre-printed check list should be used to ensure that every detail is complied with. This would normally be the subject of a meeting of departmental heads so that a full understanding is obtained. Finally, the exception rule must not be forgotten and an inspection carried out. Many managers have reason to regret omitting to do this.

The question of giving written instructions must also be considered, although unnecessary paperwork is something to be avoided. However, in most cases, telephoned or verbal instructions are rarely adhered to because they are forgotten or misinterpreted and cannot be referred to later. Therefore, memos or other forms should not be discarded out of hand as 'added bumph'. They can make all the difference between a successful or an unsuccessful organisation.

DECISION-MAKING

The most fundamental management responsibility is problem-solving and decision-making. The ability to make the right decision at the right time is worth paying for in terms of management staff. This is not a natural gift but must be learned in most cases from past errors or successes.

There is no doubt that the courses of training in the subject* offered by certain companies are a great aid to management staff, stressing a rational approach to problems and decision-making, thereby minimising the occurrence of problems. The main theme of the training is the adoption of a systematic approach which, if followed, will generate a correct decision in the light of known circumstances. It is not the purpose of this book to outline this approach, except in so far as it applies to the work of food and beverage management.

It is postulated by those experienced in the field of decision-making that problems of two types may be recognised: (*a*) those that manifest themselves as deviations from the course of normal events; and (*b*) those caused by external forces (government, economic conditions, suppliers, guests, etc.).

Deviations from normal events

If the mechanism used to monitor the achievement of objectives (responsibility accounts, job specifications and inspections) shows that a deviation is apparent, it becomes much easier to solve.

*KEPNER, C. and TREGOE, B., *The Rational Manager*, McGraw–Hill, London (1962)

For instance, should profit levels not attain financial objectives set, or procedures not be adhered to, a problem is apparent and a maintenance job must be done to bring performance back into line.

Problems caused by external forces

This type of problem is more difficult to deal with, principally because its effect is not monitored by the organisation's objectives, and when it occurs little warning is given.

For example, when SET increased costs it became a problem and a deviation from performance, in that departmental labour costs rose. However, because the problem was not generated internally it was unlikely that internal action could solve it adequately. In fact, this type of problem could be solved by passing the amount through to guests or by absorbing it.

Should the organisation be operating at a reasonable rate of efficiency, it will not be able to absorb added costs without affecting profitability. Alternatively, it may increase its tariff to offset the amount, which could result in an unacceptable price structure to its clientele.

Procedure

The procedure adopted to deal with problems differs for either type and will be governed by the following steps:

DEVIATIONS

(a) Definition of the problem in financial and procedural terms.

(b) Problem-solving. This involves determination of the change in the organisation's procedure which resulted in the occurrence of the problem.

(c) Decision and action. The problem-causing deviation must be brought back into line.

(d) Maintaining action. The deviating section must be checked upon to ensure that the problem does not recur.

EXTERNAL PROBLEMS

(a) Determination of the exact effect of the problem in financial and procedural terms.

(b) Determination as to whether it may be solved by increasing productivity internally. The results should be compared with inter-hotel comparison or any other alternative internal action.

(c) Determination of the addition necessary to the price structure to offset the amount.

(d) Determination of the effect of such price structure on the market.

(e) Decision-making and action-taking.

Making incorrect decisions costs money which is a good reason why a systematic approach is necessary to minimise them.

CONTROL FUNCTION

Because food, liquor and cash are amongst the most desirable items in terms of pilferage or fraud, the food and beverage manager must bear considerable responsibility for controlling the income and costs of his departments. The criterion of control is to make deviations from set objectives apparent, e.g. by procedures such as food and liquor gross profit levels, so that swift action may be taken to correct them. Control procedures are, in fact, problem-solving tools whose worth should be assessed, and any which do not assist action should be dispensed with.

Food and beverage controls

To consider control procedures properly it is necessary to isolate objectives in terms of those factors which affect costs in the food and beverage departments (*Table 1.3*). This, of course, is a very broad view of the controls involved and the various types in use in the industry will be discussed in detail in later chapters.

SELECTION OF STAFF AND THEIR DEVELOPMENT

The labour policy of some companies is to engage the highest calibre personnel they can afford. Unfortunately, such personnel are few, and the hotel and catering industry is too well aware of the attitude that quantity rather than quality is all that is required. Such policies naturally affect the organisations which adopt them. Staff of low calibre must reflect upon the establishment which employs them and management must learn to be as competitive in their selection of staff as in their promotion of custom.

This statement is particularly pertinent to the food and beverage manager whose department is the most technical and scientifically orientated of all hotel departments. Therefore, the selection and development of high-calibre personnel are essential to his success and the success of his departments.

It is surprising how many caterers will avoid employing a good chef at an extra ten pounds per week, thus ignoring the fact that he

Table 1.3 Food and beverage controls

Objectives	Control
Departmental profitability	
Food departmental profit	Responsibility accounts
Beverage departmental profit	Responsibility accounts
Prime costs	
Food cost	Food costing system
Liquor cost	Liquor costing system
Wages costs	
Departmental wages	Responsibility accounts
	Wages report
Staff turnover	Turnover report
Departmental costs	
Food department expenses	Responsibility accounts
Liquor department expenses	Responsibility accounts

could double the chance trade in their restaurant by producing well-presented dishes of high quality. This is not to say that one must always pay highly for competent personnel, but the level of selection of staff depends largely upon the corporate objectives and policy. In the light of this it must be decided what are the objectives of each member of staff and what price must be paid for the necessary calibre to discharge such objectives. These selection factors are summarised in *Figure 1.5*.

When an operation is commenced with a view to long-term success, it is fundamental that staff are employed who are likely to remain for long periods. It is interesting to note that one caterer who holds the views expressed above has a staff turnover of 10% per annum which compares favourably with the normal turnover of 200–300%.

As well as receiving a reasonable rate for the work done, staff are interested in developing their work skills. Employers wishing to keep staff must retain their interest by helping them develop their skills, thus achieving better performance, promotion and job satisfaction. It is always surprising to learn that many employers do not appear to realise the latent ability of their staff and do nothing to develop it. As the HCITB now apply a compulsory levy for training there is no excuse for not developing the qualities of one's staff. Moreover, free advice is always obtainable from officers of the board.

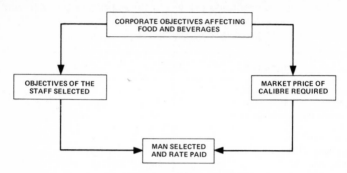

Figure 1.5. Staff selection factors

It is appropriate here to record the comments drawn from a letter from an assistant manager after attending one such training course. It must be said that he had had no formal training whatsoever, and management principles was a very new subject to him.

Dear Sirs,

I should just like to thank you so very much for your recent course which you enabled me to attend. I must say I am quite converted to the ideas that you have to offer and am very much in favour of the courses that you are now running. I must admit I was very much impressed. You might be interested to know that I have just written to M . . . . C . . . . . . and informed him of the same. I am curious as to what the reaction will be.

I hope the opportunity will arise when I can again attend one of your courses as I am sure it will be of great benefit to my career.

Yours sincerely, . . .

This is, of course, not only relevant to managerial personnel. Housekeepers, head porters, chefs and the like have benefited enormously from development of their personal skills.

The management of food and beverage departments is the most technical and complex job in the hotelkeeping and catering trade—it is, however, the most stimulating and rewarding. In most large hotel corporations food and beverage management is the launching pad to general management, as work done in administering the operation is indicative of potential in unit management. It must be clearly understood that food and beverage managers are *not* assistant managers. They are departmental managers in their own right and it is essential that they are allowed to fully administer all staff reporting to them.

2
Market research

Before setting up a food and beverage operation it is important to be sure that what is intended to be served is acceptable to the people to whom it is served. Again, this may appear to be fundamental, but it is interesting to note the number of operations which do not survive because little attention has been paid to this essential.

Market research is a method of finding out what market exists for a particular product so that it may be developed with a good chance of attracting the desired market. The procedures are very simple and capable of being utilised by any person to valuable effect.

The basic objective of market research exercises on food and beverage operations is to ascertain:

(*a*) The right people and their numbers who will buy.

(*b*) The price they will pay.

(*c*) The place where they will buy.

(*d*) The location of the right place.

ISOLATION OF MARKET POPULATIONS

The first basic task is to discover what market population exists in a particular area; this is known as a catchment area (see *Figure 2.1*). The catchment area of a particular location denotes the distance which people will travel in order to enjoy the products of an enterprise. This will differ in varying cases depending upon geographical location, and whether the operation is in a town or in a sparsely populated area. Obviously, the same conditions do not apply to operations with an artificial market, such as motorways or air terminals, where passing populations may be assessed by different means.

The limits of a catchment area are governed by a number of factors:

(*a*) Reasonable driving distance.

(*b*) Public transport facilities.

(*c*) Competition.

(*d*) Natural or man-made barriers.

Reasonable driving distance

In most areas, the idea of driving for more than 20–30 minutes to and from a meal is unacceptable. Therefore, the method of determining the catchment area is to drive out from the focal point (restaurant) along all main routes during pre-meal periods to see how far one can travel in this time (*Figure 2.1*).

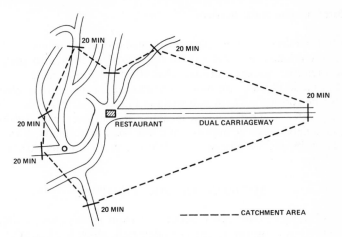

Figure 2.1. Defining a catchment area

There are other factors in particular locations which should also be assessed. They are concerned with the transient trade which may exist in the area, such as tourists, conference delegates, and sales representatives. Also, there are situations where food and beverage operations have supporting roles. Examples of this may be theatre restaurants and the like.

Public transport facilities

Where popular catering establishments are concerned, it is important
to consider carefully the location of termini, bus stops, etc. A restaurant situated at the opposite end of the town to the bus station,
for example, will find that this is reflected in its sales between 9 p.m.
and 10 p.m.

Top-quality operations also cannot ignore this when situated in
provincial towns, as proximity to the railway station may materially
affect the choice of would-be customers entertaining friends from
out of town.

Competition

Location in a catchment area may be seriously affected by competitors who could be more conveniently or centrally located in the
area, and careful consideration should be given to this point.

Natural or man-made barriers

Natural barriers, such as sparsely bridged rivers, hill ranges, lakes,
etc., may divide a possible catchment area. Newcomers to such an
area, therefore, should consider what effect these may have.

Man-made barriers are more difficult to appraise as they cannot
always be foreseen. These will include motorways, flyovers, urban
freeways, etc., which discourage local travel from one area to another.
Included here would be bypasses and link roads which have dramatic
effects on businesses relying to a great extent on transient trade.

SOCIO-ECONOMIC GROUPS

Population figures are easily obtainable from local publicity offices
and directories. However, one consideration which is often ignored
is that differing geographical areas have proportionately different
socio-economic groups. By this is meant the divisions of population
by work done and salary earned.

The socio-economic grouping considered average for the UK is
shown in *Table 2.1*. Obviously, the percentage proportion of population in Bethnal Green of a particular socio-economic group will not
be the same as that in Highcliffe, Hampshire. Therefore, a method
of isolating differing socio-economic groups must be considered in

Table 2.1 Socio-economic groupings for the UK

Group	Definition	% of population
A	Doctor, barrister, solicitor, town clerk, etc.	4
B	Surveyors, executives of medium-sized businesses	8
C	Civil servants, bank clerks	17
D	Skilled and semi-skilled workers	64
E	Unskilled workers	7

order to obtain rational market population figures. This may be done by utilising the indices of retail spending power calculated by some market research organisations for all geographical areas in the UK.

EXAMPLE: COMPARISON BETWEEN NOTOWN, NOSHIRE AND LONDON S.E. 45

Average population socio-economic group A   4%

Retail spending norm   100

	Retail spending	*Population*
Notown, Noshire	145	60 000
S.E. 45	95	45 000

Therefore, socio-economic group A in Notown contains

$$\frac{145}{100} \times \frac{4}{100} \times 60\ 000 = 3\ 480 \text{ persons}$$

Similarly, socio-economic group A in S.E. 45 contains 1710 persons.

Both sets of figures would be decreased by the number of persons in the upper age ranges according to the total age mix of the population, and by the ratio of children to total population in the area. The example shows how total populations may be reduced very critically, which is perhaps an indication why areas (even well-to-do) cannot adequately support many haute cuisine restaurants.

To summarise, socio-economic groupings of population may be assessed by the following points:

(*a*) The population of the catchment area.

(*b*) The retail spending power per head.

(*c*) The population by age range.

(*d*) Competitors within the catchment area.

In addition, in order to incorporate transient visitors, detailed research must be carried out to assess:

(e) The total passing population.

(f) The socio-economic groups in which they fall.

(g) The age ranges relevant to the population.

By dividing the resulting population assessment by the number of competing establishments in the area, the available market for each may be ascertained. From this, the revenue generated can be determined.

Assessment of market population is one of the most important stages in food and beverage market research. It is interesting to note the way in which an apparently large population dwindles when assessed as an available market which is prepared to buy.

SITE AND LOCATION ASSESSMENT

Although the population figures might indicate the success of a particular operation, it is essential to assess carefully the site and location of the operation. With regard to towns, there are three basic shapes to be considered: the rectangle, the semi-circle and the square (*Figures 2.2–2.4*). In addition, the characteristics of other population centres will also be discussed.

The rectangle

Growth in population will occur along main roads or railway lines which follow the length of the town. Therefore, food and beverage operations should be sited along the main route in order to enjoy easiest access from the maximum population. Operations, particularly those directed towards popular catering, will tend to enjoy greater patronage when sited within the outer sections of the town (*Figure 2.2, A and C*). In those areas, it will be found that the greatest number of people will need to travel the shortest distance to the site.

The semi-circle

This shape (*Figure 2.3*) is typical of seaside resorts or lakeland towns, and normally has the town centre at the waterfront, from which the main routes radiate. Secondary centres are built alongside

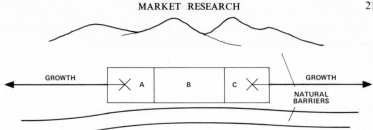

Figure 2.2. The rectangle

these routes. The importance of this structure is the consideration that sites just outside the town in position X have as much, or more, chance of attracting the maximum population as sites in the town centre, for the following reasons:

(*a*) They are equidistant from secondary areas and from the town centre.

(*b*) There is easier travel from secondary areas.

(*c*) There is probably easier parking and access to the site.

The square

Square towns (*Figure 2.4*) are characteristic of steady development over flat areas. Towns of this shape tend to enjoy focal points where the roads intersect, i.e. at the town centre (reminiscent of Roman development). Because of the evenness of growth and the ease with

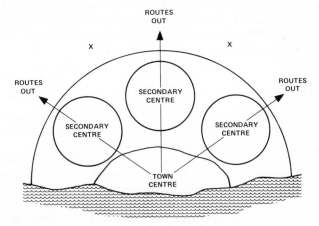

Figure 2.3. The semi-circle

which all populations travel to the centre, suburban development will be slight and unlikely to succeed to any degree.

Out-of-town sites

Because out-of-town sites cannot draw from a condensed population they normally owe their existence to being either specialised high-quality eating places or artificially attracted markets, e.g. motorway services.

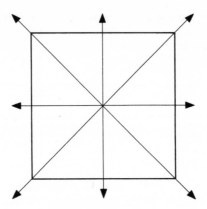

Figure 2.4. The square

The success of the former will depend directly upon continuously maintained high standards and promotional expertise. This is discussed in detail in later chapters. The success of the latter, on the other hand, is dependent upon the volume of passing traffic and the use of promotional devices such as road signs to divert the traffic.

Secondary areas

It is important that caterers should be able to isolate secondary centres. In towns of 100 000 population and upward they are located about a mile from the town centre.

Most secondary areas are old and worn out and serve populations merely as convenience centres. Traffic moves through the area on the way to other centres. American experience shows that secondary centres tend to atrophy. Therefore, caterers contemplating operations in these areas should consider the likelihood of redevelopment in the short term.

MARKET ASSESSMENT

Having decided that the site and location are acceptable in terms of population and catchment area, a detailed examination of the area must be undertaken. The examination will include the following points:

(a) Tour of the catchment area to isolate business houses, private residences and competition.

(b) Visit to all competitors in order to note:
  (i) the popularity of the establishments,
  (ii) particular areas in which they excel.

(c) Consideration of the rate of passing traffic and fluctuations in volume at different times of the day and week.

(d) Car-parking problems.

(e) Evaluation of economic level of residences in the catchment areas.

From the planning department of the local authority and the Chamber of Commerce, the following information will be available:

(f) Trends of population and industrial growth.

(g) Estimates of tourism and conferences.

(h) New development within the area.

(i) Interviews of likely patrons.

From the above data, the following may be calculated:

(a) The most desirable type of service and production for the proposed project.

(b) The number of covers for which to plan.

(c) Expected rate of seat turnover.

(d) Anticipated cover receipts.

This information can then be compiled into a schedule of income (*Table 2.2*).

Estimates of food and beverage income in hotels will, of course, be based upon overnight guests to a large degree. However, the format tabulated can also provide the basis of food income schedules for hotels.

The methods advocated here are used in varying degrees of sophistication to produce market feasibility studies. Capital has never been cheap, however, and may be prohibitive even if it is obtainable. Therefore, potential operators should examine the market very stringently to ensure that the proposed investment is capable

Table 2.2 Schedule of income

Meal	No. of seats	Turnover	No. of covers	Average cover receipts, £	Daily sales, £	Operating days	Annual sales, £	Sales mix
Luncheon	42	1·2	50	1·25	62·50	312	18 876	20
Dinner	42	2	84	1·75	147·00	312	45 864	40
Total annual food sales							64 740	60
Estimated total annual bar sales (including wine)							25 896	40
Total annual food and drink sales							90 636	100

of generating sufficient income to be viable. Although a reasonable amount of work is involved, it is a small price to pay in terms of the loss which might be incurred through abortive investment.

CASE EXAMPLE: MARKET RESEARCH—MOONSTONE RESTAURANT

Introduction

This report was commissioned by Mr. X, a Director of *Moonstone Restaurants Ltd.*, during a meeting at which Mr. J. J . . . . of this company was present, held at 8 p.m. on 6th November, 1971.

Terms of reference

The following terms of reference were stated by Mr. X at the meeting noted above:

  (a) To establish the market available to a restaurant located in Chester Terrace of the type envisaged.

  (b) To establish the minimum and maximum profitability of the operation with specific regard to its location and market.

  (c) To establish the feasibility of the establishment in the light of invested capital.

Method of operating

This market research survey was carried out by our consultants in the light of the requirements of the known business activity projected by *Moonstone Restaurants Ltd.* The activity was described as a 'Turkish-style restaurant', specialising in the service of shish-kebabs prepared upon a charcoal grill.

Catchment area

The maximum travelling distance is shown within the encircling line marked on the map in *Figure 2.5*. Pedestrian limits are shown within a one-mile radius, and driving distances are within the outer border.

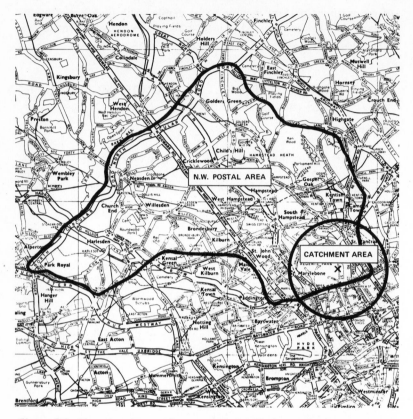

*Figure 2.5. Map showing catchment area: (a) X shows the restaurant site;
(b) outer dark lines represent the catchment area (reproduced by permission
of Geographers' Map Co. Ltd.; Crown Copyright)*

WALKING

The map clearly indicates the main thoroughfares from which
business would accrue.

DRIVING

The Greater London Area has a population of approximately ten
million, of which 930 000 are resident within the catchment area
marked.

ASSESSMENT OF MARKET POPULATION

Calculation based upon the retail spending power shows that the proportion of the population of socio-economic group A within the catchment area is 2·84%.

$$\frac{284}{10\,000} \times 930\,000 = 26\,412$$

The average family size in the UK is 2·6 persons. Consequently, the populace of the area has been reduced by an amount

$$\frac{6}{26} \times 26\,412 = 6\,095$$

Therefore, the adult population of group A is approximately 20 317, say 20 000 potential guests.

Key traders

There are *no* key traders in Albany Street. Therefore, traffic travels through it rapidly without stopping. This would indicate that Albany Street is a secondary area and enjoys very little transient trade. Key traders in the area are located as follows:

Great Universal Stores	Tottenham Court Road
Marks and Spencer	143 Camden High Street
	Baker Street
F. W. Woolworth & Co. Ltd.	242 Marylebone Road
	115 Camden High Street
	20 Tottenham Court Road
Boots	179 Camden High Street
	5 Euston Road

Private residences

The site is situated in a residential area which has been recently redeveloped. Private residences fall into the following groups:

(*a*) Mews houses, £35 000–£45 000.

(*b*) Three-bedroom flats, £3 000–£4 000.

(*c*) Flats on 99-year lease, £8 000–£10 000.

(*d*) Extensive council housing development.

The first three groups are inhabited by people who are in socio-
economic group A. The last is inhabited by people who are in socio-
economic groups C, D and E, which is not relevant for the purposes
of the survey.

Business houses

The business houses in the area are situated for the most part in
the areas of Camden Town and Portland Street (*Table 2.3*).

Enquiries were made to assess two areas relevant to the restaurant
site:

(*a*) Albany Street Barracks.

(*b*) Albany Street and Euston Road Corner Development.

ALBANY STREET BARRACKS

The Army are vacating these premises in the near future, but plans
for the site are undetermined, as was revealed from enquiries to
Camden Council and Camden Planning Department. However, it is
considered highly likely that the barracks would be replaced by
residential accommodation—probably council flats or houses.

EUSTON ROAD CORNER

The site which is now under development will contain a high proportion of commercial interests, which would be of great value to a
restaurant situated in the area.

Car parking

Albany Street is a restricted parking zone until 6 p.m. The only
other available space is in Chester Court, but it is reserved. This is
particularly relevant to the potential luncheon trade, indicating that
diners have no option but either to walk or ride by taxi.

Competition

Because of the existence of the market in the centres of Hampstead,
St. John's Wood and some parts of Camden, it is important to

consider the rival establishments in the area (*Table 2.4*). The proposed restaurant should be capable of attracting the catchment of 20 000 from the restaurants listed in the table.

As the proposed restaurant is of a speciality nature it is likely to appeal to a minor proportion of the socio-economic group,

Table 2.3 Business houses in the study area

Banks	
Barclays	119 and 215 Baker Street
	23, 161 and 293 Euston Road
	15 and 56 Great Portland Street
	179 and 190 Tottenham Court Road
Finance for Trade Limited	13 Marylebone Road
Lloyds	140 Camden High Street
	190 Great Portland Street
	18 Wigmore Street
	263 Tottenham Court Road
London Trustee Savings	160 Camden High Street
Martins	236 Tottenham Court Road
	174 Marylebone Road
Midland	90 and 186 Baker Street
	42 and 176 Camden High Street
	25 and 159 Great Portland Street
	31 Euston Road
	237 and 138 Tottenham Court Road
National	189 Camden High Street
National Provincial	69 Baker Street
	156 Camden High Street
	95 Tottenham Court Road
	23 Wigmore Street
United Dominions Trust	199 Marylebone Road
Westminster	133 Baker Street
	166 Camden High Street
	125 Great Portland Street
	Mornington Crescent
Williams Deacon's	171 Tottenham Court Road
	Marylebone Road
Post Offices	
	165 and 303 Euston Road
	111 Baker Street
	4 and 202 Great Portland Street
Insurance Companies	
Liverpool Victoria	152 Camden High Street
Emil Bloom	91 Baker Street
Alliance	24 Wigmore Street
Canada Life Assurance	5 Wigmore Street
Eagle Star	88 Baker Street
Imperial Life Assurance	32 Great Portland Street
	90 Tottenham Court Road

and it is particularly relevant to note that the *Cock and Lion* in Wigmore Street has a charcoal grill and is well rated in tourist

Table 2.4 Rival establishments in the study area

Name	Style	Address
Light of India	Indian*	59 Park Road, N.W.1
London Steak House	Grill	116 Baker Street
Quality Inn	Grill	128 Baker Street
Angus Steak House	Grill	13 Marylebone Road
Barque and Bite	Haute Cuisine*	Prince Albert Road
Chiltern	Haute Cuisine*	Baker Street
Cock and Lion	Charcoal Grill*	62 Wigmore Street
Flanagans	Old English Cuisine	100 Baker Street
Gattopardo	Haute Cuisine*	Wigmore Street
Hiroko Japanese	Japanese*	Wigmore Street
Hook, Line and Sinker	Fish Restaurant	73 Baker Street
Alpino Restaurant	Italian*	102 Wigmore Street
Copper Kitchen	English	34 Eversholt Street
Double Six	Popular	66 Eversholt Street
Green Parrot	Haute Cuisine*	62 Camden High Street
Le Petit Jardin	Haute Cuisine*	Prince Albert Road
Old Kentucky	Grill	1 Euston Road
	Grill	54 Tottenham Court Road
Oslo Court	Haute Cuisine*	Prince Albert Road
Sardar		60 Tottenham Court Road
Tandoor Mahal	Indian*	321 Euston Road
White House	Haute Cuisine*	Regents Park
Paganis	Italian*	40 Gt. Portland Street
Prince of Wales	Haute Cuisine*	Hampstead Heath

*Restaurants considered to be in direct competition to the proposed restaurant. This illustrates that in the catchment area there are 14 direct competitors as well as numerous competitors in Soho and Chelsea.

guides. Nevertheless, it has also a conventional kitchen as it cannot solely rely upon sale of items prepared on the charcoal grill.

Market assessment

INCOME

In order to arrive at an estimation of the number of diners and sales figures, the following was assumed to be the average tariff of the proposed restaurant (page 32).

Table 2.5 Market assessment

	Poor	Normal	Good
Luncheon			
Seats	30	30	30
Turnover	0·5	1	1·5
Covers served	15	30	45
Price	T^*, £ 1·25 × 10 $A\dagger$, £ 2·17½ × 5	T, £ 1·25 × 20 A, £ 2·17½ × 10	T, £ 1·25 × 30 A, £ 2·17½ × 15
Income	12·50 10·87½	25·00 21·75	37·50 32·62½
Total	£23·37½	£46·75	£70·12½
Dinner			
Seats	30	30	30
Turnover	1	1·25	1·5
Covers served	30	37	45
Price	A, £ 2·17½	A, £ 2·17½	A, £ 2·17½
Income	65·25	80·47	97·87½
Total income/day	88·62½	127·22	168·00
Annual total food income	27 653	39 696	52 416
Total liquor income at 33⅓% of food	9 214	13 220	17 456
Annual total income for food and liquor	£36 867	£52 916	£69 872

$^*T$ = table d'hôte. $\dagger A$ = à la carte.

(a)   Table d'hôte luncheon, 3-course business lunch at £1·25.

(b)   À la carte luncheon, 3-course:

	Average price
Starter	40p
Main course	£1·37½
Dessert	40p
Total	£2·17½

(c)   À la carte dinner, 3-course:

Starter	40p
Main course	£1·37½
Dessert	40p
Total	£2·17½

The assessment has been made at three levels, poor, normal, good, on the basis of a restaurant having 30 covers, open for luncheon and dinner (*Table 2.5*).

WAGES COSTS

Table 2.6 shows the wages costs.

Table 2.6 Wages costs

Establishment	Gross pay, £	Payroll burden, £	Total staff costs, £	Depart- ment costs, £
Administration				
Manager × 1 × £1 500 p.a.	1 500	300	1 800	
Cashier × 1 × £750 p.a.	750	300	1 050	2 850
Restaurant				
Waiters × 3 × £750 p.a.	2 250	900	3 150	3 150
Kitchen				
Chef × 1 × £1 750 p.a.	1 750	300	2 050	
Assistant chef × 1 × £1 250 p.a.	1 250	300	1 550	
Wash up × 2 × £500 p.a.	1 000	600	1 600	5 200
Bar and wine				
Barmen × 1 × £1 000 p.a.	1 000	300	1 300	
Wine waiter × 1 × £1 000 p.a.	1 000	300	1 300	2 600
Total staff cost	£10 500	£3 300	£13 800	£13 800

PROFITABILITY

Table 2.7 shows the profitability of the project.

Table 2.7 Profitability estimates

	Poor		Normal		Good	
	£	%	£	%	£	%
Sales						
Food	27 651	100	39 694	100	52 416	100
Liquor	9 217	100	13 231	100	17 472	100
Total sales	£36 868	100	£52 925	100	£69 888	100
Cost of sales						
Food	11 091	40	15 880	40	20 960	40
Liquor	4 608	50	6 615	50	8 736	50
Total cost of sales	£15 699	42	£22 495	42	£29 696	42
Gross profit						
Food	16 560	60	23 814	60	31 456	60
Liquor	4 609	50	6 616	50	8 736	50
Total	£21 169	58	£30 430	58	£40 192	58
Wages	13 800	37	13 800	26	13 800	19
Net margin	7 369	21	16 630	32	26 392	39
Expenses						
General expenses	1 203		1 203		1 203	
Administration	400		400		400	
Heat, light, power	1 380		1 380		1 380	
Advertising	920		920		920	
Total	£3 903	12	£3 903	8	£3 903	6
Control level	3 466	9	12 727	24	22 489	33
Fixed costs						
Rent, rates	2 000		2 000		2 000	
Other additions	800		800		800	
Depreciation	500		500		500	
Repairs	500		500		500	
Total	£3 800	10	£3 800	7	£3 800	5
Net profit/loss	(334) Loss	(1)	8 927 Profit	17	18 689 Profit	28

Conclusion

In view of the factors isolated above, it is considered unlikely that
the restaurant will be able to generate the sales shown as normal,
and, therefore, alternative means of utilising the site should be
considered.

3

The 'meal experience'

TOTAL EXPERIENCE

Unlike most products and services the meal or leisure experience is peculiar in that it derives its success from providing more than just a physical product, i.e. food and drink. It is a total atmosphere, composed of food, drink, surroundings and people, combining to form a 'living establishment'. This is described at length in *The Marketing of the Meal Experience* by Graham Campbell-Smith, and applies to most catering and leisure operations, e.g. restaurants, hotels, holiday villages or camps.

This chapter considers the components of the meal experience in order to allow the caterer to appraise all the aspects of the living establishment. Such components as food, liquor, service, design and other customers are all bound together by a common theme so that the establishment provides a total environment for those within it.

A simple way to illustrate this point is to consider the menu, hostesses and meal trays produced by airlines. Frequently, the package is not uniform. For example, an elegant menu may be produced with a daintily painted flower on the cover accompanied by a dark brown tray containing several different brands and grades of china. The whole is handed to the recipient by a hostess in a stark, dark-blue uniform. The result is an unrelated 'hotchpotch' which cannot create a good impression.

Obviously, the meal package must be considered as a whole, whether it is a cover in a restaurant or an airline tray. Items requiring consideration in the presentation are as follows:

Tray	Colour, material, shape, convenience to customer and caterer, texture.
Cutlery	Silver, stainless steel, plastic, wooden, pattern, style and durability.
Cloths	Size, colour, shape, texture, textile and durability.
Table mats	Size, design, colour, shape, material and durability.
Glass	Size, design, shape, durability and convenience.
China	Size, design, shape, durability, colour and convenience.
Condiments	Size, design, colour and convenience.

The package is, of course, distributed by service of some kind and it is important that the type of service and the attitude and clothing of the waiters or counter hands are compatible with it. If, as in many four or five star hotels, traditional elegance is the order of the day, then scruffily dressed waiters with dirty fingernails (even if they wear tails) will immediately destroy the image. Also, the meal package and service are enclosed by the walls of the establishment and it is the designer's task to convey the image and mood of the restaurant through the design, blending, of course, with the service and meal package.

The caterer should always remember that the image of the establishment must be immediately apparent to customers. It is also important to bear in mind the effect of the restaurant or hotel front as an image to passing traffic.

The whole package should be summed up in a brand name which will describe the establishment, so that potential customers are instantly aware of its function, e.g. *Golden Egg* (breakfast foods), or *Epée d'Or* (Shishkebabs).

OBSOLESCENCE

The increase of eating-out operations experienced by this country in the last few years has encouraged many caterers to change the concept of their operations frequently, to exploit competition by constantly providing novelty. This mode of operation necessitates that the cost of new concepts should be returned within the operational period.

EXAMPLE

	£
Cost of restaurant	20 000
Annual profit	5 000

The restaurant was operated for the first three years in a manner similar to that when purchased, yielding a total profit of £15 000. A change in design concept was made in the fourth year amounting to £6 000. Therefore, the restaurant is required to return an added profit and capital repayment over the life of the new concept.

	£
Required additional profit 25%	1 500
Capital repayment over 4 years	1 250
	2 750
Original return on capital	5 000
Total expected return for the 4 years of new concept	7 750

Profit and capital repayment criteria necessitated by this mode of operation indicate that the design and décor of the operation should be planned in accordance with its life. This is especially pertinent when considering soft furnishings, floor coverings, kitchen equipment, etc.

MARKETING REQUIREMENTS

A list of marketing requirements which must be considered in relation to the meal experience is shown in *Table 3.1* and discussed in detail below.

Alternatives

The customer will consider the time he has to spend over his meal. Whilst some people are willing to spend long periods over meals, one does not like to think that one may be kept waiting. Therefore, it is unwise for a restaurant to project the image of lengthy meal periods. In order to obviate this, many eating places arrange that service staff put some small item before the customer as soon as he or she sits down, e.g. ice water.

The customer will also consider alternative eating places when deciding where to eat, and this will, obviously, reflect his mood or the reason for the meal. However, the restaurateur can project his image to the customer in ways likely to make the establishment more attractive than those competitors who are promoting a similar type of meal experience.

Initial customer contact

The customer will consider using the operation in either one of two
ways: by being stimulated to make use of by promotion or recommendation or as a passing customer who 'likes the look of the place'.

Table 3.1 List of marketing requirements

Potential customer's ability to choose between alternatives
Timing of meal
Length of time taken over meal
Facilities offered by the restaurant
Mood of restaurant
Unique selling points

Facia
What is it required to say?
Will it portray mood?
Will it identify with the market?

Mood	
Social	Offer of a particular class consciousness?
Age	Portrayal of a specific era
Novelty	Offer of a particular basic food or some other gimmick
Conformity	Standard accepted operations
Escape	Fantasy
Independence	Self-service
Dependence	Degrees of service
Formality	Degrees of formality
Music and entertainment	

Customer's senses
Observation
Taste
Smell
Feeling
Hearing

Value for money

The facia is all important to both methods of attraction in that
through its design it encourages customers to enter. The pre-booked
customer may still go somewhere else if the operation does not appeal
to him from the outside; the transient will not stop.

The facia, therefore, has several objectives which are part of the
design concept:

(a) It must welcome the customer.

(b) It should intrigue (most do so, but without the welcome).

(c) An indication of what is taking place inside should be apparent.

(d) The facilities of the operation should be recognisable from the facia.

(e) An indication of the likely cost should be apparent.

(f) It should be designed with the market sector in mind.

MOOD

The mood of the restaurant is the basic design concept envisaged by the caterer, and manifests itself in the total living establishment. Many caterers misunderstand 'mood', believing it to be a 'gimmick'. However, most gimmicks do not conform to customer needs as many unsuccessful operations have proved.

NOVELTY

A novelty operation is one which is new and probably makes use of a particular staple food, e.g. *Berni Steak Houses*, *Golden Egg*.

The novelty mood must be seen to relate to the whole concept. A décor which is entirely unrelated to the food or service will serve to make the customers irritable and uncomfortable.

CONFORMITY

Conformity characterises an operation which does not attempt to provide anything new but 'plays safe', utilising some mood which has had proven success and which customers may use safely. This is an example of the use of brand image in catering.

ESCAPE

Some operations are designed to provide an escape from the rigours of life, by providing a modern or fantastic mood. It creates an unbelievable atmosphere where outside life may be forgotten, e.g. *The Chelsea Drugstore* and certain discothèques.

INDEPENDENCE

This is achieved by self-service for those persons who have no objection, or indeed prefer to help themselves. An example of this may be seen at the *London Playboy Club*. Presumably, the management believe that those persons who choose to become members prefer to help themselves to their food.

DEPENDENCE

Dependence involves the degree of service provided to customers. This may be either plate service, semi-silver service or total silver service.

FORMALITY

The degree of formality provided by an establishment will differ in accordance with the mood the caterer is trying to achieve. For example, the impressive formal silver service of many restaurants is entirely suitable for business entertaining; a more relaxed and informal atmosphere is required for young men entertaining their wives or girl friends. A good example of relaxed atmosphere, together with silver service, is to be found at *Nick's Diner*, in Fulham.

Customer's senses

Caterers often forget that customers have five senses which convey to them the contrived mood of the restaurant and other facts which the caterer would prefer the customer not to observe.

OBSERVATION

The customer will notice a number of things subconsciously or consciously when he enters a restaurant, and the longer he spends in the restaurant the more apparent these observations will become. He would probably find difficulty in explaining his feelings, but they will be present nevertheless.

The whole concept will be considered; if items or design appear unrelated they will be noticed. The many components of the meal experience must harmonise to provide totality as well as providing contrast to retain interest. Colour is important since it promotes, among other things, the creation of mood and identification of objects or areas.

TASTE

The food composing the meal experience must provide the customer's sense of taste with the following:

(a) A reasonable intensity and quality of taste (a pertinent factor when considering frozen food).

(b) A balancing of the four taste groups to provide balanced flavours within the meal—sweet, sour, salt and bitter. This will provide variety and contrast.

SMELL

The restaurant should be free from smells caused by bad ventilation and air circulation, and which are not part of the meal experience. Many public houses having bar snacks have lost trade because the bars, which have not been ventilated for cooking, hold cooking smells. Other restaurants overlook the importance of eliminating stale cooking aromas and lose custom.

FEELING

The customer's sense of feel is vitally important. His progress from door to bar to table must be uncluttered and clear. No customer wants to weave around tables as one is often invited to do. Involuntarily touching objects or people, or being touched, is found irritating or offensive by most people.

The table setting will occupy a customer's hands for some period. Therefore, the items set on it should be pleasant to the touch. In this category are included the following: paper, plastics, some types of tiling used as table tops, certain man-made fibres and various kinds of metal and glassware. The shape of the items is also important. A way-out set of cutlery may look attractive but if it does not feel comfortable to hold its objective is defeated. This applies to certain shaped glasses, condiments, etc.

HEARING

The customer, if seated by himself (as is likely in popular restaurants), will hear the sounds of the establishment; diners in company will only hear background sounds beyond their conversation. Because of this, most restaurants provide a musical background which, apart from assisting atmosphere, drowns background noise. Music, therefore, becomes important and its intensity, together with its nature and tempo, must be carefully considered in relation to the meal experience. Frequently, the background music makes communication with waiters very difficult and serves only to irritate customers. Therefore, it should be arranged that conversation at a distance of at least eight feet can be plainly heard above it.

Value for money

The price in relation to the meal experience must be such that it is acceptable to the market. Value may differ with markets, as in cases where restaurants charge too little to be acceptable as well as others charging too much. An important consideration in relation to value is the consistency and appearance of the food served. A customer having a bad meal will remember that he paid the same price for a better meal previously.

DESIGN

A cardinal rule of food and beverage operation design is that there must be a genuine belief on the part of the caterer himself in the experience he is providing. There is little point in a caterer providing an establishment full of 'gimmicks' in which he does not really believe, as his market is unlikely to believe in them either. One does not have to look far, especially in London, for operations thrown together in the misguided belief that any gimmick will attract the market. This criticism is especially true of some of the staple food based operations which followed the steak house fashion. It is wrong to provide a gimmick which will create mood or atmosphere without realising that mood is created from the totality of the operation and not from isolated items within it.

The design totality receives its guidelines from the definition of the meal experience laid down by the caterer. The definition must be as exact as possible because all the components of the experience will be decided upon with direct reference to the definition, which takes the form of an expanded main business objective.

These ideas can be illustrated by describing a restaurant planned in London based upon 1920 décor and operating theme. Because of the varying moods of the 'twenties it was important that the exact mood desired was carefully defined for planning and operational specifications. The caterer in question wished to create the mood of sentimentality, pathos, even sickly sweet to depict the sadness of an era suffering childish hysteria on the one hand and the attitude and feelings of 'the bright young people' on the other.

It was essential to select a name which would convey the above without encouraging an unnecessary image of 'the roaring twenties'. After careful deliberation and constant reference to the definition above the name *Bitter-Sweet* was decided upon—a definite culinary connection strongly indicating the mood the restaurant was attempting to create.

Subsequently, each component of the restaurant was measured against the definition above, as was the totality as it gradually progressed. By ensuring that every component incorporated into the theme had a natural and authentic base being free from gimmick or anachronism, a mood compatible to the definition was finally established.

A framework must be provided, therefore, to guide the design approach so that the maximum benefit may be derived from it. This is outlined on the following basis.

Market research

Market research should be undertaken to decide whether there is a market for the type of operation envisaged and the size, area and age range involved. The price range also has to be considered and the question of whether added facilities may be incorporated in the operation.

Meal experience

The experience the selected market wishes to enjoy should be described in detail. This will become a statement of intention of what the operator wishes to do.

Design concept

From the above an abstract plan of the 'living establishment' may be formed which, when thoroughly agreed and finalised, may be the basis of a designer's brief.

A caterer caters and a designer designs. On no account should a designer be permitted to exceed the brief either in terms of concept or budget. One rarely finds a designer who is capable of confining himself to the brief. However good one thinks one's design is, it is always better to revert continuously to the original concept and insist that it is discharged without deviation. For example, the job of the designer is to provide the design of the restaurant facia but unless the caterer stipulates exactly what is required he may finish up with a gold medal design which does not appeal to his market. Perhaps two of the finest facias designed are those of *Sands* and *A Taste of the Twenties*, both in New Bond Street.

There are a great many caterers who have allowed building costs to rise unhalted with little to show for it now. One frequently comes across designers who insist on undertaking the total brief, from door knobs to deep fat fryers. Undoubtedly, some may be excellent but most cannot possibly have a detailed knowledge of every field involved in a food and beverage operation and, therefore, the utmost care must be exercised if this is intended.

On the other hand, the caterer is not a designer and should consider the advisability of designing his own operation with great care. Apart from the aspect of talent, a professional designer has the continuous opportunity to examine new fabrics, materials, and design ideas which a caterer would not normally enjoy.

Budget

When the design brief has been finalised and before a designer is instructed, a financial appraisal should be undertaken incorporating the budget costs allocated to the cost of building, equipping, decorating and opening the operation.

Completion of operation

If the results of the financial appraisal are acceptable, the professional will be instructed. It is advisable to construct a programme at this stage of development to monitor the timely and effective construction of the operation. The programme would probably consist of activities together with a series of meetings to clear up outstanding matters and to preface the next stage of activity. A continuous financial control would be exercised to ensure that the operation did not exceed budget. Included in the programme would be other necessary items such as the planning of promotion, employment of staff, and planning of administrative procedures.

The above has outlined a broad programme for the formulation of the design but it is pertinent to discuss one or two points in greater detail.

The bar

If in a high-priced operation there is likely to be some wait for tables, then the bar must obviously be placed as near as is practicable to the entrance. The design should also take into account the requirements of 'chance' customers who wish to find out whether a table is available without being obliged to hover about a crowded restaurant as so often happens.

The caterer should consider the above through the eyes of the customer entering the establishment and not so much for his practical requirements. Effective design is often a compromise between effective layout and customer appeal, and should a decision be necessary the rule is, 'the market comes first'.

Normally, where a catering operation is built into a shop there is not a great deal of choice but it is surprising what can be done with a little thought (*see Figure 3.1*).

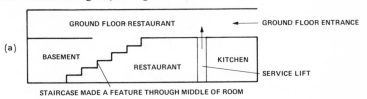

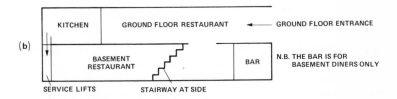

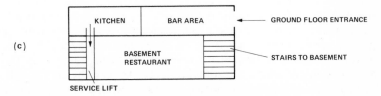

Figure 3.1. Examples of restaurant layouts

With a new building, of course, there are obvious advantages both in terms of marketing appeal and efficiency and, as may be seen from the diagrams, there is plenty of opportunity to devise something with originality. This is basic design which contributes the basis of mood and can then be further embellished by decoration. Should a particular feature be required to illustrate a design point to create mood (atmosphere) then careful consideration must be given to basic design in order to achieve it through shape. For example, consider *Figure 3.1(a)*. The centre stairway of the restaurant allows the opportunity to build a landing covered by a canopy supported by columns, designed in a Persian style (*Figure 3.2*). In this way a design feature is constructed which adds shape and dimension to the room design. The design of a room should generate from

Figure 3.2. Persian-style stairway design

its shape, and if its shape is unsuitable it should be changed. Embellishment merely looks contrived and fussy and, therefore, unappealing to the customer.

Tables and chairs

Many caterers complain that a chair smaller than they now use is not available, and if it were it would provide more covers. The reason for this is that most chairs are designed around the human body and there is a minimum criterion below which manufacturers will not go unless a special order is placed.

By utilising smaller chairs and tables, a larger number of covers may be installed in a room. A high density, however, often affects the atmosphere, particularly if the restaurant is in a basement or internal room where there is no access to external light. The rule governing seating is simple: if there are not enough covers in the room to achieve adequate profitability the room is not big enough. The question of space is one which should be tackled at the planning stage when the meal experience is conceived, and should be governed by it. The caterer ceases to be objective when he alters his plans to incorporate further seating, as he is then tampering with his product specification.

Seating arrangements tend to sort themselves out with use when tables are movable, but where tables are fixed the layout must be carefully considered. There are two aspects, as indicated in *Table 3.2*.

Table 3.2 Criteria of layout for seating

The customer	The waiting staff
Tables Wide enough for a full cover and forearms and elbows (a common mistake is to order tables before considering the size of the full cover)	*Tables* Ease of access between customers or for plate service, serving across one side of the table which is not laid up
Chairs Comfortable for medium to gourmet, not so comfortable for snacks to medium price	*Chairs* Straight-legged to avoid trip-ups
Both Ease of access, away from possible jostle from waiting staff and other tables	*Both* Clearly defined and adequate service channels

A scale drawing incorporating total service requirements should be made. The drawing will include all items such as table mats, table lights, cutlery, condiments and other table decorations as well as tables, chairs and access space. Realistic estimates should be made for waiters and waitresses carrying flats and plates, and using trolleys, by actually doing the job and measuring the space necessary.

Uniforms

An often forgotten item when designing restaurants is the provision of suitable uniforms. Frequently, this is remembered too late and conventional uniforms are purchased or other items are used which will do. The staff are as much part of the totality of the operation as any single physical component and they should be decorated in a suitable manner.

This section has laid down the principles of design and mentioned some of the pitfalls that are likely to occur. A systematic approach is required for any exercise, and especially of the design concept, as this is probably the largest single expenditure a caterer is likely to undertake.

4
Planning the menu

Menu planning is one of the most complex of marketing exercises undertaken in catering, and like the planning of all products should be designed according to certain criteria:

(a) It must satisfy a market need.
(b) It must comply with the total meal experience.
(c) It must not be too extensive.
(d) It should enable the target gross profit to be achieved.
(e) It should not encourage waste.
(f) It should be balanced.
(g) It should be exciting.
(h) It should be within the culinary range of the kitchen staff.

There are other factors to take into account when planning the menu. However, those listed above are a selection of the most important.

SATISFACTION OF MARKET NEED

This falls into a number of areas which are of prime importance to both customer and caterer.

Overall menu theme

The fact that the menu should have an overall theme as well as providing variety might be thought to be a contradiction in terms. However, for practical purposes both needs must be satisfied.

A menu which does not indicate totality in accordance with a central idea is discordant, appears disconnected and thus fails to satisfy the customer. The reason is that the customer does not consider the components of his meal, i.e. starter, main course, etc., as separate entities, but as a whole. Therefore, if any part of the meal from menu presentation to petits fours is inconsistent the whole is spoilt; it is essential that the menu on presentation is seen to be a totally acceptable product whatever the customer finally selects from it. The total meal experience/living establishment concept gives the guideline here. As has been said, the design of a food operation involves the capture of a particular mood and the menu should be an integral part of that mood rather than something added on afterwards.

A good example of a very appropriate menu was in the *Soup Bowl* in Dublin where, in fact, there was no menu! The dishes were presented verbally by waitresses carefully trained to describe each dish and its method of preparation.

The restaurant was of the bistro type producing a few dishes well. Therefore, a short menu, comprising a choice of three main courses, was what was expected.

Further, a selection made upon a customer/host relationship is an obvious extension of the atmosphere. *Nick's Diner* achieves the same effect by presenting a menu containing down-to-earth chatty descriptions of the dishes.

Examples of operations which do not achieve a totality are widespread. Two common examples are:

(*a*) Restaurants indicating haute cuisine or French cooking by the name or facia whose menu is composed of steaks and grills only.

(*b*) Small hotels (and not so small) whose image indicates one of home cooking and whose menu consists of unrecognisable variations of classic dishes. Usually, they are preceded by the inevitable 'fruit juices various' and followed by the even more inevitable—variations upon the theme of ice cream.

Component dishes

The component dishes should be relevant to the menu theme but should also appear exciting to the customer. This is probably one of the most difficult things to achieve. The selection of menu items is one which, if properly approached, will take some time. Good restaurants are often remembered by particular dishes which they offer because they are different or better than elsewhere.

Many interesting ideas may be tried without necessarily resorting to Saulnier (which everyone else uses anyhow) like oyster-burgers, or variations on national dishes to make them more palatable to the market. Not many people sell tortillas, for example, which are simple to prepare and delicious to eat.

An interesting menu is shown in *Figure 4.1* and was designed for a bistro operation. It achieved both excitement and anticipation.

Menu price

In marketing terms this is, of course, extremely important. The menu price is governed by value for money and competition.

A few restaurants manage to remain full, despite competition, even when meal prices are appreciably higher, because the food served is much better and represents value for money to the customer. This is, of course, a factor which must be considered objectively because it is difficult to find fault with one's own product. It must, however, be done periodically.

The menu price must be well within the reach of the identified market. Many caterers have overestimated the potential average bill with disastrous results.

COMPLIANCE WITH THE TOTAL MEAL EXPERIENCE

Too often restaurants are designed and built expensively, to be spoilt by a menu which does not conform to the requirements in terms of total meal experience. Much of the success of Mario and Franco's restaurants was due to the identification of the interior design with the menu. This is particularly important when considering transient customers who will make the decision during or after their meal whether or not to come again. If they cannot reconcile the menu with the design and the mood it creates, they will not be at all impressed.

A London discotheque serving meals at £3 per head enjoyed a large membership but sold very little food, because the atmosphere and the price encouraged the guests to believe that the meal would be compatible. The menu was very limited, consisting of a few simply prepared dishes which did not maintain customer interest. Consequently, although the club had many members, very few of them dined.

Bistro Menu — Pop Style

Soups: Iced Lebanese soup   Scrambled eggs soup
Soupe à l'oignon gratinée   Peasant soup

Cold hors d'oeuvres: Cold trout in white wine   Smoked mackerel fillets
Pâte maison   Egg mayonnaise   Vegetable vinaigrette
Tarramasalata   Ceviche Mexicana

Hot starters: Mussels in batter   A potted shrimpburger
Grilled sardines

*   *   *   *   *

For a light luncheon or supper dish (or, alternatively, for an enormous breakfast or tea) :
Our own range of freshly cooked pizzas, thin pancakes or omelettes — all served with salad and ranging, in fillings, from seafood to tomatoes to mushrooms. Specifically, we recommend :

A plateful of cold meats, baked potatoes and salads
A truly meaningful cornbeef hash and salad
Free-range eggs and sweetcured bacon
A great frankfurter or two
Fettucini verde Mam Mia con Insalata
or,
The great American hamburger and salad

*   *   *   *   *

Main courses:

Colonel Frobisher's very special kedgeree
Chicken in a salt crust
Your actual barbecued spare ribs
Choucroute garnie Alsacienne
Charcoal grilled pork chops, served with apples
A roasted rack of lamb
Charcoal grilled kebabs, full of Eastern promise
Filet de boeuf en croute

Dish of the Day: served from the trolley, Boiled Silverside of beef, carrots and dumplings

All main courses are served with an appropriate selection of fresh vegetables

*   *   *   *   *

Puds, etc.:

Apart from a selection of cheese and fresh fruits, we have :
Chocolate marble cake and cream
Meringues and fresh fruit salad
Organically grown yoghurt
A range of ice creams and salad
Brown Betsy and cream
Baked apple and cream
Cheesecake 'Moyshe Dayan'

*   *   *   *   *

Coffee and sweeties

Figure 4.1. Example of an interesting menu (courtesy Nick Clarke)

THE MENU MUST NOT BE TOO EXTENSIVE

An extensive menu will require more stock, there will be more likelihood of mistakes and more risk of confusing the customer than a shorter menu consisting of well-cooked meals.

THE MENU SHOULD ENABLE THE TARGET GROSS PROFIT TO BE ACHIEVED

Many caterers demand certain profit percentages on their food operations, but they seldom investigate the cost of producing the menu, which creates an inevitable variance from the target.

All dishes on the menu should be costed to take into account the actual cost of food served, i.e. inclusive of bones, trim and other wastage. There is no point in hoping for a 65 or 70% gross margin if it cannot be achieved, because the chef will merely be frustrated by management demands and, eventually, tend to ignore them.

The menu whether à la carte or table d'hôte should be carefully priced as above, 5% cost tolerance added and the selling price computed from the total:

Grapefruit cocktail	5p
Fillet steak, etc.	50p
Sweet	4p
Coffee	$1\frac{1}{2}$p
	$60\frac{1}{2}$p
add 5% tolerance	3p
Total cost	$63\frac{1}{2}$p
Target gross profit	= 60%
Cost of meal	= $63\frac{1}{2}$p

Selling price $= \dfrac{10}{4} \times 63\frac{1}{2}$p $=$ £1·59, say *£1·60*

The above calculation is straightforward as far as à la carte menus are concerned. Table d'hôte menus are slightly more complicated.

From any range on a table d'hôte menu there will appear a lowest cost meal and a highest cost meal. The caterer hopes that this will average out in terms of cost, but he cannot always be sure. Supposing it was intended to serve lunch at 75p from the combination below:

Starters: 5p   Sweets and coffee are common to all meals.
4p   Therefore, there is a fixed cost of $6\frac{1}{2}$p per
$2\frac{1}{2}$p   cover. Starters and main courses provide
$7\frac{1}{2}$p   the variable.

Main course:

$12\frac{1}{2}$p	Highest starter cost	$7\frac{1}{2}$p	Lowest starter cost	$2\frac{1}{2}$p
	Highest main		Lowest main course	
15p	course cost	$17\frac{1}{2}$p	cost	$12\frac{1}{2}$p
$27\frac{1}{2}$p		25p		15p
	Add fixed cost	$6\frac{1}{2}$p		$6\frac{1}{2}$p

Sweets:

5p	Total cost	$31\frac{1}{2}$p	$21\frac{1}{2}$p
	Add 5%	2p	$1\frac{1}{2}$p

Coffee:

$1\frac{1}{2}$p	A $33\frac{1}{2}$p	B 23p

A   Cost at $33\frac{1}{2}$p $= 44\%$
B   Cost at 23p $= 30\%$

It can be seen that A is 4% over the target cost of 40%. Therefore, either alternative dishes must be provided to reduce the cost per meal, or the caterer should accept the excess cost, hoping to recoup the difference on other selections, e.g. B at 30% showing a 10% saving on the accepted cost per diner. The difficulty here is that a comprehensive cost control must be exercised in order to define whether losses are due to inefficiency or to the way the menu is written. A safer method, which obviates extensive cost control, is to ensure that all menu items of whatever combination yield the target gross margin or more. A disadvantage of balancing out is that customers tend to choose the most expensively produced dish on the menu, and the menu is likely to run over cost.

THE MENU SHOULD NOT ENCOURAGE WASTE

The menu has a cost control function as well as a marketing function, and the menu writer (this term refers to any person who carries out the duty, not to a specific functionary) in his zeal to provide variety and satisfaction of market needs, should not run the risk of losing financially by not utilising stock on hand or unused items in the kitchen.

Also, it can be a temptation to offer items which have not been sold a number of times in different ways in order to conserve cost. This, of course, can be extremely dangerous. For example, a college canteen produced pre-cooked steak and kidney pies which had been warmed up two days running on the counter hot cupboard. On the third day the meat was removed from them and used for shepherd's pie. These practices resulted in a very high incidence of sickness in the college.

What is in the store?

It is essential that menus allow stock to be rotated quickly. It is not unusual for large consignments of specific goods to be purchased at considerable saving only to find that they remain in the store for long periods. If it cannot be used, do not buy it; if it has been bought, use it or sell it. In any event, the menu should not be written without due consideration of the items in store. An idea of the stock position, as well as items which are semi- or fully-prepared, should be continuously updated by the menu writer on a daily basis.

Market trends

Close contact with the market must be maintained by arranging the provision of alternative price lists and studying the trends, as well as observing the price indices published in some of the catering magazines.

This function calls for close co-operation between the menu writer and the buyer, so that the best practical compromise between economics and marketing may be adopted and continuously manipulated to suit the changing situation.

Fruits of the season

Seasonal changes affect availability of goods quite drastically. Menu writers should be aware of this, although the majority seldom acknowledge that there is any variation. At least, so it would seem from the narrow range of vegetables offered during some seasons of the year.

Some items are considered mundane and tend not to be included, although they may be plentiful and reasonably priced. Imagination should be used to incorporate seasonal variety into the menu, in the same way as certain unusual dishes might be incorporated to arouse interest.

THE MENU SHOULD BE BALANCED

The menus, whether à la carte or table d'hôte should be capable of satisfying a wide variety of tastes. As many combinations of dishes as are offered will be served at one time or another. Menu balance will be achieved by ensuring that:

(a) Differently priced foods are featured in each section.

(b) Textures and dish composition provide ready alternatives.

From the two basic rules above, a huge variety of menu items may be planned in a balanced form, e.g.:

Starters
         Meat (2)   Fish (2)   Fruit (2)   Egg (1)   Pasta (1)

Main dishes
         Meat (2)   Fish (2)   Egg (1)   Pasta (1)

Sweets
         Fruit (2)   Cake (2)   Pastry (2)   Ice cream/sorbets (3)

Although the above does seem simple, and is obvious, it is surprising how many menus one comes across which do not achieve balance of any kind.

Variety of dishes may govern to a large extent the number of repeat visits by customers to an establishment. There is little point in having a wide choice of main courses, unless the balance of the menu allows complete variety in the selection of total meals rather than having to put up with 'old faithfuls' in the starter and sweet sections.

THE MENU SHOULD BE EXCITING

Much of the anticipation of the meal is generated by the design and composition of the menu. For example, grapefruit cocktail or a portion of melon will not induce great excitement. Neither do the items have to be exotic or rare delicacies which might frighten the customer. One is striving for the unusual, the touches which make the menu different from elsewhere. In the menu shown in *Figure 4.1* few of the dishes are very unusual; they have merely been conceived in a way which will interest the customer. One or two caterers are becoming very adventurous, producing good food which is exciting to look at and eat, but which is merely a variation of the theme found in most restaurants and hotels.

It is a mistake to think that imagination and variation is the province of expensive restaurants only. It is just as important, if not more so, for lower-priced operations, which are more prone to menu fatigue, to attempt imaginative and exciting production.

THE MENU MUST BE WITHIN THE CULINARY RANGE OF THE KITCHEN STAFF

Having produced a menu conforming to all the provisos discussed above, it is, of course, self-evident that the kitchen should be able to produce it as it was originally conceived. This may be taken into account either by training, if the staff are skilled and receptive enough to absorb the new concept within a reasonably short period, or by starting the process of menu planning again, recognising the limitations of the staff. One would, of course, hope that a caterer would not allow himself to be in a position where he could not improve his product, because of the lack of skill at his disposal.

5
Menu marketing

Having selected the items to appear on the menu with due regard to the envisaged market, the next step is the production of the menu. Many good restaurants fail in their menu presentation because they ignore the simple rules of menu marketing. These become especially relevant if the menu is likened to a catalogue or brochure which is used by the market to select the products it desires. There are not many business concerns as privileged as a restaurant where the customer is 'captive' as soon as he enters the premises. The menu is an example of advertising media which every customer is obliged to examine carefully, and its presentation deserves the most detailed consideration.

MENU DESIGN

Very few caterers are designers and, therefore, they should always consult one when producing promotional media. A design which might be considered very attractive may appear to the customer to be old-fashioned, out of balance, oppressive or childish.

As the basic purpose of a menu is to enable the customer to read it and, in so doing, make a selection, the prime objectives in menu design are clarity and legibility. Menus (particularly à la carte) in this country usually consist of a double or single page. Extra pages serve only to confuse the customer and slow down selection time. Occasionally, the back page may be used as a selective wine and drink list.

The printing of menu items should be clear and have at least double-line spacing. If, as often happens, they are crowded together, the customer's eye may pass over them, especially in a darkened room. The caterer should test his menu for legibility by reading it in every part of the room. This will ensure that both printing and lighting allow the customer to read it without strain.

Hotels and restaurants use a variety of processes to duplicate menus. All, with the exception of the offset process, tend to produce indistinct smeared copy and errors due to careless typing. Good restaurants often fail in this respect and it is pointless spending considerable sums to provide a prestige front to the customer when it can be so easily destroyed by an error in the menu. Many printers will either tender a reasonable price for printing a daily menu or insert, or photocopy and print (offset) from a carefully typed and checked menu supplied by the catering operation.

Because the menu is an example of advertising literature, it is essential that all relevant information be included upon it, especially since it may be removed by customers to show to friends. Such information should incorporate:

(a) Times of opening.
(b) Days closed (if any).
(c) Banquet and party facilities.
(d) Any other supplementary services.

Changing the menu

Menu format and items should be changed reasonably frequently, i.e. about twice annually, to retain customer interest, and it is suggested that à la carte menus should be changed every three months and should reflect the season. From the customer's point of view, it is extremely embarrassing to order an item which is out of season. When seasonal changes are made, it is a good idea to alter the cover design also in line with the contents.

MENU ITEMS

The question of English *versus* French menus tends to manifest itself at every food and beverage discussion. But, here, it is pertinent to discuss this point purely from the marketing aspect.

Basically, the customer requires to know what products are being offered and what they comprise. The public does not know every dish and every garnish; consequently, choice from a French menu may be only guesswork. The customer may obtain what he wants.

But, if served with something he does not expect and does not like, he will feel irritated, especially if he notices another customer being served with something which looks delicious. If the menu item has to be written in French because there is no English equivalent, e.g. Petite Marmite Henry V, then a description of what is actually presented should be included in the menu.

There are a number of ways of making menu items interesting. Instead of using the normal sub-titles, such as 'Starters' or 'Appetisers', 'Fish', 'Entrees', etc., some descriptive imagination may be used. For example, a cold buffet with a sea flavour could be:

'Casting Off'	Starters
'In the Net'	Fish
'The Captain's Table'	Entrees
'Weighing Anchor'	Sweets

Other course names designed to whet the appetite would be, 'Salad Suggestions', 'Sizzling Platters', 'Dessert Delicacies'. Descriptive names may also be used to describe dishes. However, one must be sure that what is offered is actually served. For example, if Wiltshire Ham is offered, it must be Wiltshire Ham.

Menu fatigue

Restaurants presenting the same menu day after day will suffer menu fatigue and customer boredom, even if the restaurant has no competitors. Therefore, they must offer a reasonable variety in their produce. This applies whatever the location.

One famous restaurant in London was recently sold to become a steak and liquor bar operation. It was situated in the most popular eating area in the West End and should have been full every day. The custom was, however, sparse and was due to the fact that the same very limited table d'hôte and à la carte menu was offered for over two years without change.

The menu writer should consult with others for suggestions, etc. Otherwise, over a long period, he will begin to run out of new ideas, and, in any event, customers will tend to anticipate the menu. This will, obviously, preclude surprises and variety.

RESTRICTED MENUS

Apart from pleasing the caterer himself, there is no other reason for offering large menus. They have few advantages and many disadvantages. For example, they tend to:

(a) Confuse the customer.

(b) Make dish selection take longer.

(c) Overburden the kitchen.

(d) Cause preparation and presentation to suffer.

(e) Increase waste.

(f) Yield many by-products which have to be off-loaded in 'made-up' dishes.

Special chef's dishes

Very few food operations advertise special dishes which are the chef's *pièce de resistance*. Most businesses, however, have a leading product and this also applies to well-known restaurants. But, caterers are normally reluctant to publicise a particular speciality.

The advantage of this type of publicity, however, is in its role as an 'image builder'. The object of the exercise is to present to the mind of would-be patrons a reputation for a particular food, so that when the dish comes to mind so does the eating place. Examples of eating places creating this type of image are:

Simpsons in the Strand	English Fare
Hunter's Lodge, Broadway, Worcestershire	Fondue
Wheeler's Restaurants	Lobster, Oysters
Rib Room, Carlton Tower	Steak
Epée d'Or, Gt Cumberland Place	Shishkebabs

FACTORS TO BE TAKEN INTO ACCOUNT IN MENU MARKETING

Price

It is very easy to consider price in isolation and reflect this in the quality of produce, without considering the market or its choice in terms of value for money. But, it would be incorrect to postulate that all operations should be market-based. Obviously, there are some market situations where price creates stringent guides to the operator. These are, for the most part, popular catering establishments, which consist of a population obliged to watch its purse. Operators, therefore, have to decide very carefully the type of food and size of portions they can afford to sell.

Gross profit

Consideration of price inevitably leads to consideration of gross profit. In the UK, most three- and four-star hotels and restaurants aim for around 65% of sales. The rate of gross profit set is determined by four factors:

(a) Value for money.

(b) Competition.

(c) The rate at which seats are turned over.

(d) Wages and other costs which require to be absorbed by gross profit.

Examination of a sample of gross profit levels (*Table 5.1*) shows that the lower the price the lower the profit level, although a marked drop in gross levels is noticed in very high-priced operations.

Table 5.1 Example of profit levels attainable

	Haute cuisine restaurant		Cafeteria	
	Average income per cover £3		Average income per cover 37½p	
	£	%	£	%
Sales	24 000	100	24 000	100
Cost	8 400	35	12 000	50
Gross profit	15 600	65	12 000	50
Wages, etc.	8 400	35	4 320	18
Overheads	3 600	15	3 600	15
Net profit	3 600	15	4 080	17

Table 5.2 shows the gross profit economics of food operations, but it is not definitive and there are, obviously, many exceptions. It is, however, an indication of the gross profit characteristics of the hotel and catering industry.

Table 5.2 Gross profit economics of food operations

Type of operation	Gross profit level, %
Industrial catering operations	20–30
Industrial catering and low-priced cafeterias	40–50
Low-priced restaurants and hotel food operations	45–55
High-priced restaurants and hotel food operations	45–60
Average for restaurants and hotel food operations	60–65
Banqueting and outside catering	70

Food quality

It is essential that the initial article is of good quality. Certainly no amount of garnish or preparation will improve it further. This important topic is dealt with at length in Chapter 6. Basically, however, the rule is: 'To measure the optimum specification resulting from price payable and quality available, and to ensure delivery and use of that specification only.'

Much of the quality problems of food operations are due to the kitchen and restaurant service of food, and it is fundamental that both departments are able in terms of skills and equipment to provide the specified quality. This is particularly relevant to the food and beverage manager in his role of menu maker. Many restaurants advertise menus to which they cannot do justice, and would do far better if they publicised a plainer menu which could be produced well.

Design concept of the restaurant

It is important that the design concept of the whole operation is reflected in the menu so that it is not a weak link or becomes a break in the sequence of the meal experience. This has already been discussed in detail in Chapters 3 and 4.

Dish analysis

Of considerable assistance to the food and beverage manager is a daily analysis of meals taken, whether the operation is table d'hôte or à la carte. In fact, this is an integral part of any worthwhile food cost control system and is discussed further in later chapters. The relevance to the menu planner is two-fold:

(a) Compilation of menus to accommodate the tastes of the market.
(b) Elimination of heavily fluctuating cost-mix of menus resulting in low gross profit.

The average bill

It is important to know how much customers will spend in a particular operation, and the ranges of expenditure they choose to incur.

From this information, the food and beverage manager can plan à la carte menus to suit the largest sector of his market.

These data are also essential when considering the use of loss-leader items to encourage diners to use the restaurant. There is little value in encouraging diners to choose loss-leaders, which they will never discard on subsequent visits. A loss-leader should appear a bargain, but not so much of one that the customer will not be persuaded to try something else.

6

The back door

In many establishments, receipt and checking of goods is not considered important, and, in most, this is reflected in the quality of raw materials and gross profit. There seems little point in setting careful specifications for goods and negotiating price and quality with suppliers, if there is no check to ensure that these specifications and prices are adhered to; goods of any quality and price will be accepted—and thus become acceptable.

The objectives of the receiving department are to ensure that:

(a) The quality and price of goods which have been *ordered*, are *received*.

(b) Delivered goods are delivered in total according to orders made.

(c) Substitute deliveries (if any) are suitable for use.

It is not the purpose of this book to outline the various frauds which occur in and around food and beverage operations, save to note that there are many, and intelligent use of the systems described here will prevent such frauds occurring.

THE RECEIVING OFFICE

The site of the office should be as near to the back door as possible, although where this is impracticable, it should certainly be situated between the back door stores, kitchen and cellars. An essential piece of equipment is an adequate scales, with a large double-faced dial. The existence of scales is not enough—the clerk must be able to use them properly, they must be easily accessible and in good working order. Every unsealed item should be weighed, i.e. meat, fish, poultry, etc., to ensure that shortages are made known.

Because of the amount of documentation involved in the receipt and checking of goods, it is necessary that the office should be large enough and properly equipped to deal with it. Many back door offices appear to be furnished with throw-out equipment and are seldom decorated. This merely adds to the confusion and muddle of documentation. Therefore, it is important that each piece of routine equipment, e.g. trays, filing cabinets, etc., has a function and that its design is related to that function.

PHYSICAL CHECKS OF QUALITY AND QUANTITY

Most receiving clerks find that delivery men tend to use traffic congestion or parking problems as excuses for making their delivery times as short as possible. This, inevitably, gives rise to opportunities for 'dumping goods' or 'making short deliveries' if the receiver is unable to carry out a thorough check within the time available. The risk of financial loss in inefficient receiving systems demands that management must insist upon suppliers' delivery men remaining until staff are absolutely sure that the delivery is correct.

A method of underlining this, and also relieving the receiving clerk of any unpleasantness which may occur, is to erect a notice similar to that shown in *Figure 6.1.*

Deliveries to this .... must be weighed, counted and checked on arrival to the satisfaction of the company's management. Goods which cannot be checked in accordance with the above will not be accepted.

.... General Manager

Figure 6.1. Example of notice

There are two main types of goods, i.e. cartoned, branded goods and perishables delivered by weight. There are special considerations for dealing with the delivery of each type.

Cartoned or branded goods

Branded goods should be weighed, even if cartons are sealed; this is a very simple and quick task as tare weights are always quoted upon the outside of cartons.

Perishable goods

When receiving perishable goods, it is important that the clerk weighs every item of goods delivered—many food operations lose a large amount of money every year because of this laxity. He must use his skills of observation and judgment in quality checks on perishable goods. A cardinal rule in disputes concerning quality, is to ask the member of staff who will ultimately use the goods to make the final decision.

Generally, in making routine appraisals of incoming goods the clerk should make selective checks for quality by looking for dented tins, rotten or bruised fruit and ensuring that meat is in the correctly ordered cuts.

Standard orders

The purchase of materials in consultation with the user will allow specifications of ordered items to be drawn up in accordance with management policy. Thus, the receiving clerk will know what the specification of goods is before they arrive. This will be seen as the secondary stage after compiling a menu, wine, or bar drinks list, which lays down the goods necessary to discharge adequately the menu and wine lists at the expected cost.

Standard specifications may be posted up on a wall, included in a manual or incorporated upon the order for the goods. The latter method is the most preferable and goods specifications are incorporated upon what are called 'standard order forms' (SOF). The receiving clerk is passed a copy of the form on each occasion the goods are ordered, so that he knows precisely what to accept or reject when they arrive. A sample standard order form for meat is shown in *Figure 6.2.*

By specifying goods in this way it is unlikely that substitutes, wrong sizes or wrong quantities of goods will be accepted into stock.

THE GOODS INWARDS PROCEDURE

When the receiving clerk (or user of the goods) is satisfied as to quality and quantity, the supplier's delivery note/invoice will be signed and a copy retained. If the operation uses standard order forms or some other method of identifying the specification of the delivery, this will be taken into account during the checking procedure, and any differences, i.e. weight and price, noted.

Meat: Supplier: ....   Date: ....

Item	Ordered per	Order	Delivered	Actual price £p	Actual cost £p	Standard price £p	Standard cost £p
Fillet steak	lb	10	10½	0·81½	8·56	0·75	7·87½
Veal escalopes	packs (1 × 12)	3	3	1·80	5·40	1·80	5·40
Lamb cutlets	lb	5	5	0·21½	1·07½	0·20	1·00
Pork chops	lb	6	5	0·24	1·20	0·25	1·25
Sausages (pork)	lb	5	5	0·14½	0·72½	0·15	0·75
Spare ribs	lb	4	5	0·12½	0·62½	0·10	0·50
Total					17·58½		16·77½

Figure 6.2. Standard order form for meat

A record of all incoming goods should be kept by the receiving clerk, which may be a daily sheet or a goods inwards book (*Figures 6.3–6.5*). Whichever form is adopted is immaterial as they are kept for the same purpose, but it should enable one to:

(*a*) Identify the goods entering into stock for stock ledger upkeep.

(*b*) Provide a ready means of referring to deliveries.

(*c*) Provide certain accounting information, i.e. creditors unrepresented by invoices.

(*d*) Provide basic information for the calculation of trading results.

Date	Supplier	Item	Size	Price £p	No.	Bin no.	Amount £p
4.5.72	J. Bloggs	Whisky 'Students'	26 oz	2·50½	12	64	30·06
„ „ „	A. Splick	Vermouth Sweet	30 oz	0·96½	12	34	11·58

Figure 6.3. Liquor goods inwards book

The ultimate purpose of the goods inwards record will govern its format. Many operations maintain goods inwards information which is so basic that it is of no value. It is important that management considers the purpose of the information in terms of its end result and specifies that the information kept is required to provide it.

Provision should be made for filing invoices and delivery notes tidily. An alphabetical card index is useful for this, or alternatively

Date	Supplier	Item	Size	Price, £p	No.	Meat, £p	Fish, £p	Poultry, £p	Veg, £p	Bread, cake, £p
6.4.72	Breadles	Bread	Small loaves	0·3	40					1·20
6.4.72	A. Cutts	Lamb chops	6 oz	0·6½	60	3·90				

Figure 6.4. Food goods inwards book (where standard order forms are not used)

Date	Supplier	SOF no.	Meat, £p	Fish, £p	Poultry, £p	Veg., £p	Bread, cake, £p	Tea, coffee, £p	Groceries, £p	Sundries, £p	Total £p
6.4.72	Breadles	Bread					1·20				1·20
6.4.72	A. Cutts	Lamb chops	3·90								3·90

Figure 6.5. Food goods inwards book (where standard order forms are used)

an alphabetical concertina folder may be used. By this method, invoices will be kept in order and will be passed, correctly filed, to the accounts department or equivalent.

Every invoice should be stamped on filing with a stamp similar to the one shown in *Figure 6.6*. Each section of the stamp imprint

Goods received	
Entered GIB	
Checked SOF	
Extensions Checked	
Over £5 — Manager	
Passed for payment	

Figure 6.6. Example of an invoice stamp

will be signed by the relevant member of staff, when the task referred to has been carried out. Standard order forms will also be filed and passed to the accounts department at short intervals.

Occasionally, the receiving clerk will be obliged to refuse all or part of an order as it does not comply with the specifications laid down. When this occurs another document will be required, so that the accounts department can be kept informed. This form will also be used where prices or quantities on the invoice/delivery note are incorrect, so that suppliers' accounts may be adjusted. This form is called the goods inwards credit note (*Figure 6.7*) and it will be used by the accounts department to request a supplier to adjust his account.

In some cases the receiving clerk will keep a small cash float to pay for 'cash on delivery' items, carriage, etc. This will require a separate petty-cash control and recording of vouchers, all of which adds further administrative effort to the job of the clerk and the accounts department. Because of this, the cash control information is seldom adequately kept, and it is recommended that all cash disbursements should be made by the accounts department or front-office cashiers.

Finally, to ensure that the back door is carrying out its job properly it is a sound procedure for management to pass goods through the department so that random checks may be carried out.

Grand Hotel			No. 00098
....			
....	*GOODS INWARDS CREDIT NOTE*		
Supplier.................		Date....................	
Account correction			**£p**
SOF No.			
Signed		Total	

Figure 6.7. Goods inwards credit note

7
Requisitions

The purpose of adequate requisitioning is to ensure that 'every item issued from stores or cellar will be recorded and identified in terms of material weight or cash value.' In order to isolate areas of loss of materials it is necessary to account for each material moving through the operation at any point, whether it be liquor or foodstuffs. For example, Chapter 6 discusses the procedures necessary to ensure that goods ordered are delivered to the hotel or catering operation in good condition. The use of adequate requisitioning systems allows management to assess the amounts used by each department, and to balance storage stocks and consumption.

Requisitions may be of three basic types in any hotel and catering operation:

(*a*)   Food from stores.

(*b*)   Liquor from cellar.

(*c*)   Sundry items from general stores.

Two types of procedure are in current use, both of which are effective in the requisitioning of goods. These two basic types may be found in as many as twenty different forms, but all should conform to the points noted below.

GENERAL POINTS OF REQUISITIONS

(*a*)   They must be signed by *both* issuer and receiver.

(*b*)   Both issuer and receiver should have a copy.

(*c*)   Each separate item should be requested, specifically in writing, in terms of size, weight and brand name.

(*d*) All entries must be legible.

(*e*) The goods in question should not be signed for, until the receiver is absolutely sure of the items he has obtained.

PRICED REQUISITION FORMS

Many caterers are advocates of priced requisition systems (*Figure 7.1*). This means that if, for example, a bar requisitions one bottle of

Crestline Hotel			192
REQUISITION			
No.	Item	Bin	£p
4	Pink Horse	42	21·60
12	Beer	104	0·90
6	Gin	44	32·40
Issued Received	Total		54·90

Figure 7.1. Bar priced requisition form

whisky it will be charged with the selling price of approximately £5·40. Although effective in some cases, priced requisition forms are not as effective as unit control systems and will involve the caterer in considerably more work, since every requisition must be calculated and not merely the final consumption. Further, they can be used for liquor systems but not for food.

With regard to the former, however, in bar management, priced requisitions do allow the total value of each day's requisition to be recorded against the sales, and to be carried on progressively, as shown in *Figure 7.2*. This type of control system has to be operated in conjunction with par stocks and bottle-for-bottle requisitions, which are explained more fully in later chapters.

As may be seen from the figure, the control has severe limitations and is only really helpful if stocktaking is carried out twelve or

		...........................Hotel		Month ended..................	
			Cocktail Bar sales and issues		
Date	Bar sales, £p	Sales cumulated, £p	Requisition, £p	Requisition cumulated, £p	Difference £p
1	34·40	34·40	40·30	40·30	(5·90)
2	48·10	82·50	46·30	86·60	(4·10)
3	60·15	142·65	47·85	134·45	(8·20)
4	58·20	200·85	60·30	194·75	(6·10)
5	43·05	243·90	50·20	244·95	(1·05)
6	18·10	262·00	14·95	259·90	(2·10)
7	30·20	292·20	30·55	290·45	(1·75)
8	16·40	308·60	18·20	308·65	(0·05)
9	40·45	349·05	39·40	348·05	(1·00)
10	54·30	403·35	57·30	405·35	(2·00)
11	60·35	463·70	59·35	464·70	(1·00)

Figure 7.2. Bar priced requisition form showing cumulated sales

fourteen times a year. Any shorter period will not allow trends to show through stock fluctuations.

UNIT REQUISITION FORMS

Unit requisition forms (*Figure 7.3*) are the most commonly used forms in the UK. It is, however, unusual to find that forms and procedures comply with the points compiled above.

Whatever type of requisition is used, it must·be considered carefully in the light of the system to be superimposed upon it, as

Grand Hotel		108
DRY STORES REQUISITION		
Unit/wt.	Item	Bin
Issued Received		

Figure 7.3. Unit requisition form

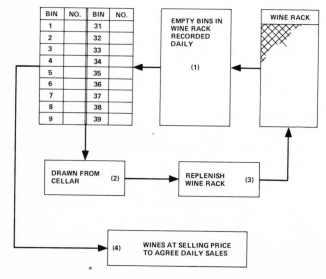

Figure 7.4. Wine requisitioning procedure

requisition procedures form the basis of all stock control systems of any hotel and catering establishment. Also, it is important that they should be correct. Thus, should particular brands be unavailable and others supplied, this fact should be noted, as well as requisitions which are cancelled because the items are not in stock.

An unusual but effective requisitioning procedure is shown in *Figure 7.4* for accounting for wine rack issues and sales based upon an imprest system.

8

Storage

All businesses must build up a buffer store of goods to obviate any risk of items not being available when required. This is one important objective of stock-keeping. It is more complicated than just the mere retention of spares, however, as it can affect the economic operation of the business drastically, if not administered efficiently.

STOCK LEVELS

The old adage, 'stock is as good as money' has a grain of truth, when one considers the relationship of money to stock:

	Current assets			
	A			B
	£		£	
Cash at bank	10 000		6 000	
Debtors	4 000		4 000	
Stock	10 000	24 000	14 000	24 000

Any increase in stock results in a decrease in cash at bank, which could place creditors and wages payments at risk.

Many managers tend to build up stocks to cover any and every situation. This leads to enormous stockholding and inevitable cash problems.

EXAMPLE

Current stock, £		Annual purchases, £
Food	6 000	60 000 at $(10 \times)$
Beverages	15 000	40 000 at $(2\frac{2}{3} \times)$

The stock turnround should be in the region of $50 \times$ for food and $9\text{--}10 \times$ for beverages.

Annual purchases, £		Turnround	Stock level, £	Stock difference, £
Food:	60 000	50	1 200	4 800
Beverages:	40 000	10	4 000	11 000
			Total	15 800

The example is slightly exaggerated to illustrate the point. But it can be seen that the stock held is grossly in excess of the unit's needs, and this is by no means unusual. In many cases, pressure may be removed from the bank account by rationalising stockholdings.

A method of establishing minimum stockholdings is to allocate a maximum stockholding to each item normally held in stock. This will take into account seasonal demand (some companies have two or three maximum stock amounts dependent upon season), delivery periods, and discounts, if any, for bulk buying.

EXAMPLE

A restaurant requires three cases of x per week, and the item is delivered weekly; a bulk discount of 10% is given for ten-case lots. The *maximum* stockholding would be four cases probably, i.e. holding one in stock and having three delivered weekly. An alternative would be to have ten cases delivered every three weeks at 10% discount. The discount must be measured against:

(a) Storage space utilised.

(b) Added stocktaking.

(c) Extra risk of pilferage.

This example will not affect the bank account as the bulk order covers only three cases, and, in normal events, the account will be payable monthly. If the cases cost £12 each, then a discount of 10% on a delivery of nine cases will be £10·80, and will probably be attractive to the caterer.

However, a bulk order may involve buying perhaps three or four months in advance, stock being payable after the first month. In this case, the effect on the bank account must be considered.

EXAMPLE

If £500 of stock is purchased at 5% discount, being enough for four months' consumption, then the cost in bank interest would be

$$10\% \times 500 \times \frac{3}{12} = £12\cdot50$$

The discount gained is £25, so a profit of £12·50 has been made. This, of course, is satisfactory, provided that the bank account will allow an expenditure of £475 in one month, which would normally be expended over four months.

Unless discounts are very attractive, bulk ordering is usually found to be an unacceptable proposition in view of the other, hidden storage costs mentioned above.

Bargains

Bargains often appear very attractive at the time. Experience has shown, however, that they generally tend to be more trouble than they are worth.

THE STORE

Apart from financial criteria, there are physical criteria which should be considered, in order to allow the store to be operated efficiently. They are comparatively cheap to install in comparison with what might be spent in other areas of the operation.

When constructing new operations it is quite easy to locate all stores close together for supervision, and to ensure effective delivery procedures and adequate space. In old operations, however, this is often difficult and the best use must be made of what is available. An ideal layout would be as shown in *Figure 8.1*. All stores would have up-and-over doors and heavy items such as meat would be carried on overhead rails running round the bay.

Food storage

Obviously, items such as meat, fish and poultry must be stored in cold rooms. However, many establishments only have refrigerator storage, which is far from adequate and into which all three items are bundled. Cold rooms are not very expensive, but it is essential that adequate planning should be done initially to incorporate enough refrigeration. This will allow sufficient space for the meat, fish and poultry to be stored properly. Hems should be placed so that blood cannot drip on to other items. Therefore, plentiful racking and trays should be provided.

In this country, vegetables and fruit can be stored in any cool room, although in hotter climates air-conditioned rooms would be necessary. The items should be spaced evenly on metal racks through which air is allowed to circulate and the room should be well ventilated.

Although the above criteria apply to any stores, in this case the provision of adequate racking is especially important. This is because the variety of dry stores goods carried tends to run to two or three

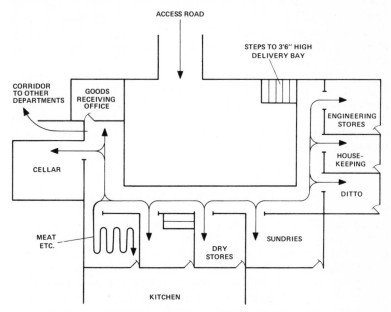

Figure 8.1. Optimum layout for stores

hundred items dependent upon the type of menu offered and it is essential to rack goods so that they may be easily found, counted and replenished.

The question of the ease of counting stock is one which is often ignored. However, when one considers the time spent by administrative staff in checking miscounts of stock, there is ample indication that it is much more economical to arrange stock initially in a manner which will allow easy counting.

Cellar

Drink should be stored in a room with a steady temperature. Any risk of fluctuating temperatures should be obviated by the installation of an air-conditioning unit which is automatically regulated.

It is essential that cellar stock should be accurately counted, and for this reason uniform racking should be used for wines, whilst spirits and liqueurs should be stored on deep shelves.

Other stores

Other items which will require storage in a catering operation come under the category of spares, i.e. soft furnishings, linen and other materials. They should be kept in warm areas so that they are adequately aired.

Silver, china and maintenance spares should be stored in any form of tidy racking, which will enable them to be found when needed and allow stores checking. It is not always realised how much cash is tied up in maintenance items and stores of silverware and china. Untidy and muddled stores result in overstocking and consequent over-expenditure.

STORES RECORDS

Two types of stores recording are in current use, i.e. 'bin cards', and the 'master stock ledger'. Bin cards are, at best, useful memoranda for the storeman or proprietor and show stock levels, deliveries and requisitions. Unfortunately, the cards have no control function as they are kept only by the storeman, and do not show the overall picture of stores transfers to other outlets in the establishment. Inevitably, invoices or delivery notes are missing, requisitions

Date	Folio	De-livery	Requisition				Bal-ance dry store
			Kit-chen	Grill	Coffee shop	But-tery	
11.1.70	Stock b/d		4	2	1	3	8
12.1.70	Delivery	24					32
13.1.70	Requisition		2	1	1	2	26
14.1.70	Requisition		1	3	2	2	18
15.1.70	Stock c/d		(2)	(2)	(1)	(1)	18
	Consumption		5	4	3	6	
15.1.70	Stock b/d		2	2	1	1	18

Figure 8.2. Master stock ledger form

are lost or forgotten and the records do not tally with the stock. One cannot expect the general calibre of personnel carrying out store duties in the hotel and catering industry to be absolutely accurate and practical experience unfortunately confirms this.

The master stock ledger (*Figure 8.2*) is a recording method which is more preferable as it gives greater control and accuracy. The ledger is kept by the control staff. Each entry is made from an accredited document, delivery note/invoice or requisition, the final stock balance being checked physically in the store.

SUMMARY

Storage is basically a matter of common sense, provided that the following requirements are catered for:

(a) Sufficient space and racking to allow quick identification of stock items, and stock checking.

(b) Relevant temperature and humidity for the type of stock carried.

(c) Adequate control records to account for all items coming in, going out and being retained in store.

(d) Stocks not to exceed the minimum necessary to adequately operate the establishment.

9
Centralised production

The concept of centralised production is one which, on first consideration, would seem to be the answer to many catering problems. To some extent it is—if scientifically carried out. In the UK, however, except for certain isolated instances, centralised production has not been popular. Concerns which are in operation at the time of writing are as follows: Alveston Kitchens; Gardner Merchant; Ford of Britain; Hospital Committee, only one of which is a truly commercial operation retailing to hotels and restaurants. Undoubtedly, the reluctance of UK caterers to centralise stems from the connection of centralisation with various freezing techniques, which are not fully understood and which appear to be very expensive.

From visits to already existing commissaries throughout the East Coast and Mid West of the United States, it has been established, that, contrary to current management opinion, the Americans are no further ahead in the use of centralised techniques than the UK. In fact, observations in this chapter are drawn as much from the UK as from the USA.

PROFITABILITY

Although catering experts have claimed that, as yet, there is no proven case for centralisation, many organisations of various sizes show substantial earnings by utilising the basic concept in their operations. This is not to say that costs are reduced for every item when treated on a centralised basis, a fact which is recognised by the various concerns which operate commissaries. For example, one very large commissary found that it was gradually eliminating production of certain commodities. The reasons prompting this were that organisations specialising in those foodstuffs could sell them to the commissary at a cheaper price than commissary production cost.

The commissary profitability depends on the following factors:

(a) *Labour*. Reduction of kitchen preparation staff in end-units.

(b) *Food cost*. Greater control over waste, and portion sizes; competitive purchasing through bulk orders; use of waste on by-production.

(c) *Equipment*. Intensive central use of heavy equipment, reducing commitment in individual units.

(d) *Product*. Ability to control product quality centrally.

(e) *Labour strategy*. Particularly valid for hotel and restaurant operations is the ability to employ staff from 9.00 a.m. to 5.00 p.m. in a commissary, as opposed to the difficulty in obtaining staff who will work shifts.

It is essential that a detailed financial appraisal be produced before embarking on a commissary operation. No general rule can be given as the profitability or otherwise depends largely upon the product, the size, number and turnover of the units, and the method of preserving the food, if any.

EXAMPLE

Group of ten restaurants considering commissary operations:

		£
(a)	*Commissary cost*	
	Rental of floor space 2 000 ft^2 at £3	6 000
	Depreciation of fixtures and fittings, 10%	500
	Depreciation of equipment, 10%	1 000
	Expenses	1 000
	Wages of 15 personnel (5 part-time)	30 000
	Total annual operating cost	£38 500
(b)	*Group cost savings*	£
	Reduction of preparation staff, 20 × 750	15 000
	Decrease in food cost, 2% × £600 000	12 000
	Decrease of annual depreciation, 10% × £5 000	500
	Total savings	£27 500
	Deficit	£11 000

The example contains fictional figures, but illustrates the areas to be examined before preparing a financial appraisal.

Commissaries must be viewed differently from conventional operations. They are factories and should be considered as such. The operations and timing are more complicated than a kitchen and, therefore, require more detailed administration than would normally be required for a kitchen.

SITE

Although some commissaries are sited in old factories, the most efficient are those which have been designed around the processes. Framfield Farm Kitchens, in Maryland, is the commissary of the Marriot Corporation and is the largest of its kind in the world, as well as the most advanced. The commissary was designed from basic principles and is housed within a building specially constructed for the purpose.

This may be compared to the Food of America Commissary which is much smaller, employing 40 staff (most of whom are part-time) preparing 18 000 meals per day. The Marriot Commissary employs some 620 staff.

Because US food habits differ slightly from those of the UK, there is no need for a wide variety of meat cuts to be produced or a fish and poultry department to be included in US commissaries. Therefore, UK commissaries would be required to add these departments to the operation without benefiting from previous US experience.

Having agreed an overall plant, the detailed layout of equipment and the type of equipment must then be decided upon. Most small commissaries prefer to have as much free floor space available as possible, so that production may be changed by moving equipment to the most effective positions. This allows maximum utilisation of items of equipment and facilitates supervision.

There are, of course, some departments which require to be self-contained. For example, cold rooms and certain preparation areas such as soup boilers and stock kettles must have a fixed position because of plumbing and trunking layouts. For the most part, preparation tables and machines should be movable so that they may be used for alternative production items with a minimum of effort. Further, to minimise space requirements many commissaries arrange that certain staff, e.g. the pastry department, work at night in what was the final packaging department during the day.

FOOD PRODUCTION AND PREPARATION

The profitability of a commissary depends, largely, on the contents of the end-unit menus. As has been mentioned, US commissaries tend to produce a narrow range of foodstuffs in keeping with American eating habits. This is especially so in meat production but is true also of other items, thus making them more difficult to produce to the requirements of the UK market. Operators in the UK must, therefore, gear their end-unit menus to the capabilities of the commissaries.

Meat production

As meat production in the US is restricted to a narrow range of cuts, a meat preparation shop would produce the following items from a purchase of selected prime cuts:

(a) Cuts from steak.

(b) Prime joint cuts for roasting.

(c) Trimmings plus second-grade meat to be used for hamburger meat and pie fillings.

(d) Bones and excess trim for resale.

It follows, therefore, that because of the greater range of involved butchery, staff in the UK would have to be more skilled than their US counterparts.

In the US, except for hamburger production, all operations visited employ butchers to trim and prepare meat and no part of the procedure is automated. There is strict division of labour, utilising skilled and unskilled personnel to best advantage, thereby minimising labour effort.

Apart from the butchers, the majority of a staff in the department are not usually highly skilled. The various processes involved in meat production can be subdivided as follows and staff are trained in each procedure:

(a) *Machine operators.* Staff operating dicing machines, hamburger-making machines, mincers, etc., to a strict procedure.

(b) *Trimmers.* Staff who are taught to trim carcasses and prime cuts.

(c) *Packers.* Staff who pack goods into foil cans, operate vacuum-packing machines, label or pack finished goods into containers.

An example of a meat department visited in New York is shown in *Figure 9.1*. The large cuts of meat are transported on overhead rails. Small special cuts and other items such as hams are delivered to butchery or packaging. Obviously, this is a large operation. Those likely to be built in the UK over the next few years will be smaller and employ highly skilled butchers. Therefore, they will be unable to use their butchers on trimming and packaging. The

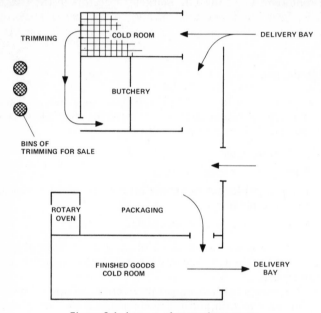

Figure 9.1. Layout of meat department

economics of the meat production will be geared to the shift production of the skilled men and the degree of butchery involved, i.e. whether carcasses or smaller cuts are purchased will be of no consequence. Intending commissaries will have to consider their forward meat production requirements and decide whether enough butchery will be required to occupy butchers on full day shifts.

Economic considerations such as these give rise to the question as to how small commissaries can be. For example, in terms of the butchery department, they may indicate to the caterer that he need not butcher, but merely portion and pack, or cook centrally. Also, of course, the economy of discount on bulk buying must be measured against skilled wages cost, or, alternatively, the savings of pre-portioning against the cost of wastage.

Vegetable preparation

In the USA, where considerable use is made of prepared, ready-mixed salads, the advantage of central preparation is evident, especially where these may be retailed to supermarkets as well as for end-units supplied by the commissary.

With regard to packs of single vegetables, careful consideration should be given as to whether they should be produced at all, and, if so, of what type and range. This is because packs of single vegetables may be purchased ready prepared from specialist firms at less than production cost, and it is probable that the small commissary will not find it profitable to centrally prepare vegetables. One reason for the relatively higher production cost is the difficulty of utilising machines to automate vegetable cleaning. For example, in potato preparation, modern peeling equipment requires, in addition, the assistance of a girl to watch for those with deep eyes or hidden blemishes in order to cut them out by hand. The same applies to most vegetables which are not easy to clean properly.

Fish and poultry

This department cannot be automated to any great degree and could be amalgamated with the meat department, if its staff are not being utilised to full capacity. The labour involved in semi-skilled manual work and the economic justification for its existence lies in the measure of portion control and savings of unit staff.

Soups

Even at a low rate of production the bulk manufacture of soup becomes a worthwhile proposition, and it is not surprising that this is usually the most scientific and production-orientated department of commissary operations.

There is a wide range of variation in the degree of sophistication involved in soup-manufacturing operations. However, all types have certain basic similarities. For example, *Figure 9.2* shows a fully automated operation controlled by a console and involving very little manual labour. The boilers are permanently fixed in position, as are the stockpots. They have automated stirring gear which may be operated at varying speeds, and are steam heated and water cooled. An intricate system of plumbing controls the routing of stock, water and other ingredients to:

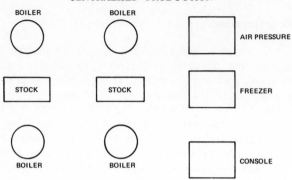

Figure 9.2. Fully automated soup-production operation

(a) Boilers.
(b) Stockpots.
(c) Packaging.
(d) Through freezer to increase viscosity (very light soups).
(e) Through air pressure to decrease viscosity (stews, etc.).

The final soup packs are one-gallon polythene bags ready for heating. Alternative methods of packaging are in metal urns and waterproof cartons.

An operation of this type requires a high level of production to be justified; this particular installation serves 250 restaurants in four States.

At the other end of the scale, an efficient operation can be planned using ordinary tip-up steam-jacketed boilers, as shown in *Figure 9.3*. The ingredients are moved by hand but for the relatively small production involved this is not a problem. Cleaning and packaging are also done by hand.

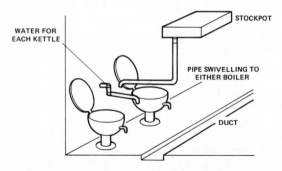

Figure 9.3. Hand-operated soup-production operation

Bakery

Most American commissaries include large bakery sections involving very heavy capital expenditure. It is doubtful whether commissaries in the UK could benefit from this department in profit terms, as items could be purchased from specialist bakers at production cost or below.

Dry goods store

Most commissaries include dry goods stores, and purchasing of the items is the responsibility of the commissary. The goods are normally delivered together with manufactured items in the normal way.

The dry goods store will be placed in such a position that it is convenient for both inward and outward deliveries as well as for the drawing off of dry stores as ingredients for commissary manufactured items.

RECEIVAL AND DELIVERY

Normally there are two loading bays, one for receiving and one for delivery. They should be adjacent to the relevant store to facilitate loading. For example, the receiving bay should be adjacent to the prime goods stores, i.e. purchased meat, vegetables, fish and poultry, and the delivery bay to the finished goods stores which contain items ready to go out to their end-units.

RETAIL SALES

Most large commissaries take advantage of the opportunity to distribute to retail shops; the two largest visited, sell 35% of their total production to stores and supermarkets. However, this is not readily available to the smaller commissary, unless the customer requires one of the comparatively small range of goods normally produced.

One danger to be avoided by small commissary operations is the production of special orders for retailers. The main objective of the commissary is to sell specific goods to end-units owned by the operating company and it would find it extremely difficult to serve two markets. Inevitably, the outside customer will complain loudest and receive more favourable attention than the end-units.

METHOD OF OPERATING

There appear to be two basic types of commissary operations, both providing specific advantages to the users.

Weekly production runs

From forecasts obtained from end-units of their forward requirements, one weekly production run is scheduled. This prepares all items of a particular type on one occasion only. As soon as the run is finished a department will produce the next item scheduled.

The advantage of this type of production is in the comparative ease with which a control system may be installed and operated. The biggest disadvantage is that in the event of an error in production scheduling, it is wasteful and costly to organise a further production run of small volume. A further disadvantage is that the method leads to the build-up of stocks, both unfinished and finished, thereby reducing commissary profitability. This method of production inevitably requires the use of heavy-duty freezing equipment.

Daily total run

This method is based upon daily needs of all items required by the end-units two days ahead. It has the disadvantage that, as the forecast gap is shorter, the end-units are not able to provide very accurate requisitions.

In addition, the method requires fairly sophisticated accounting and control as many different items are being prepared on one day, and detailed records must be made of each. Stock limits will be low, and the commissary should be able to maintain very low stock levels. Further, daily production does not require extensive freezing techniques. Large cold rooms capable of chilling food are sufficient.

ADMINISTRATION

A commissary will normally operate according to the structure shown in *Figure 9.4* which can be enlarged or reduced depending upon size and requirement.

Commissary operations are a phenomenon of the not-too-distant future and caterers with foresight are already looking ahead at the possibilities. However, the operation of a commissary requires considerably greater administrative and management skill than the industry has tended to demand hitherto.

Buying

Any organisation depending for its existence on the economics of bulk buying must pay particular attention to the process of buying.

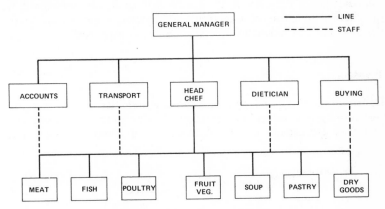

Figure 9.4. Commissary structure

The following are the main objectives of the buyer:

(a) Goods quality and price must be equated with the size of purchase order.

(b) All purchase requirements must be met.

(c) Buying practice must supplement a policy of minimum stock-holding.

Accounts

When purchase specifications have been made and the raw material components of a dish assessed by the dietician, the accounts department is in a position to produce a standard cost for the dish and its components.

The control of commissary production is normally a mixture of batch and standard costing, which is monitored by electronic means, e.g. punched card or punched tape. When a production run is initiated by the total of the orders made, the ingredients are requisitioned and put together on a pallet. In a large commissary, this is transported by means of a fork-lift truck; in a small commissary it is hand hauled. A cost card follows the pallet from stores to final production so that the actual cost of finished items may be calculated and measured against standard.

Dietician

The dietician's function is to ensure that each item produced is satisfactory in terms of nutrition and calorific value. In addition, the dietician will normally supervise quality control staff.

Transport

Distribution of goods, routing, and maintenance of vehicles are very important commissary operations. It is not surprising, therefore, that they are usually under the control of a senior manager. The

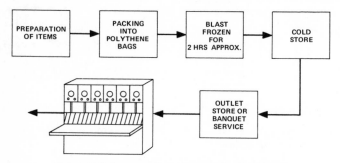

Figure 9.5. Layout of small centralised operation

complicated job of batching-up deliveries (normally weekly or bi-weekly) of as many as 200 different items to 600 locations requires considerable administrative skill in order to avoid disastrous errors.

SMALL CENTRALISED OPERATIONS

There are some very good examples of smaller centralised operations, one of which is described in *Figure 9.5*. The purpose of the installation is to provide ready-prepared food, which may be served to banquets, or supplied to the grill (coffee shop), and certain items in the commissary.

The preparation of the food takes place during kitchen slack periods, principally after luncheon service. The made-up items are put into polythene bags which contain from one to six portions. The packed items are marked with the date of packing and the name of the item, and then blast-frozen preparatory to storage. They are kept in store for from three to six months and moved on a first-in, first-out basis. However, some items cannot be stored for more than three months so a careful check must be made of the dates and stock movement. Refrigerators in the outlets are stocked up daily from the central cold store.

When an item is ordered it is reheated by a simple boiling process which operates by a timer. The cooked items are placed on the plate, the garnish and vegetables being added separately.

There are, of course, many refinements which are not included above, such as carefully calculated production schedules and coloured photographs of the dishes to guide presentation.

10
Advertising and promotion

Advertising and promotion is often confused with marketing and it is important to differentiate between the two functions. *Marketing* is the provision of the right goods to the right people, at the right time and in the right place. It is, in fact, the total control function of a business, its sole reason for existence. This has been described in detail in a previous publication.* *Advertising* is the method of *contacting* the market, informing it of the product and persuading it to buy. Some advertising campaigns are much more successful than others and therefore one must consider, firstly, the general function of advertising before dealing with the effect of each component medium.

GENERAL FACTORS

Advertising is, essentially, a means of communication. Because some campaigns obtain high results whilst others do not, it is apparent that there are factors which govern the ability of communications to contact the market. Two basic requirements are as follows:

(a) The product should be orientated towards specific market needs.

(b) The advertising medium should be considered as the shortest line of communication between product and potential customer.

* FEARN, D. A., *Management Systems for the Hotel, Catering and Allied Industries*, Business Books, London (1969).

The marketability of food and beverages has been discussed in Chapters 2 and 5, in which the reader will have considered the philosophy of tailoring the product to market needs. This chapter concentrates on the use of the various advertising methods and media, as there is considerable evidence that promotional programmes in the hotel and catering industry are not as effective as they might be.

Placing the advertising media or establishment of sales programmes requires consideration of the following factors.

Timing

The communication must be made at the right time. For example, a direct mail shot arriving on a Monday advertising a new restaurant would probably not be as successful as the same shot arriving on a Friday or Saturday morning. In fact, large retailers consider that the effect of 90% of their advertising is felt within 72 hours of publication.

Again, a food and beverage manager may wish to attract boards of directors to hold meetings and have lunch at his hotel. In this instance, as most boards meet during the fourth or first week of each month, he would be advised to time his communication to reach the company secretary or managing director by the third week of the month so that it is still of interest to the meeting.

The customer

The communication must be directed to the person who can make a decision concerning the sale. The caterer is wasting his time and promotional material unless the prospect is not only willing but *able* to buy. This applies not only to individuals, but also to collective markets in terms of advertisements in magazines and newspapers, addresses in direct mail and broadcasting populations at varying times of the day. For example, there is one well-known brewery which insists on advertising beer on television at 5.15 p.m.

Design

The design of advertising media should be the best that one can afford but this need not necessarily involve a great deal of expenditure. Normally, a complete range of the basic design is required initially, i.e. house style, notepaper, envelopes, etc. All are based upon a common theme and thus serve to create a common image to the market. Any further design of advertising media will incorporate this theme also.

Design must be compatible with the market by being orientated to the age and socio-economic group of which the market is composed, and it must also project the concept of the catering operation. For example, notepaper for international hotels is usually designed on heavyweight cream or white paper, with gold and black embossed lettering, to project the image of elegance and high living. Notepaper for a leisure centre or sporting club would indicate sun and outdoors by utilising warm browns, fresh greens and sky-blues.

Caterers who have depended on the same methods of advertising for years should consider the following facts:

(a) New ideas do not remain new for long; customers' eating and drinking habits change.

(b) The quality of food, accepted prices and methods of service vary.

(c) New methods of production and service may require testing before introduction to the market.

(d) Advertising effectiveness should be rated by some form of measurement.

(e) Share of market and financial comparisons are vital pieces of information.

(f) The market is a continuously changing combination of mixtures (ages/socio-economic groups and public taste).

PLANNING ADVERTISING AND PROMOTION

As in all aspects of business, promotion requires careful planning and budgeting.

Example: promotional plan—La Bella Vista Ristorante

OBJECTIVES

(a) To raise the average bill per diner from £1·35 to £1·50.

(b) To increase table occupancy at dinner from 0·75 to 1·50.

(c) To increase drinks per diner from 22½p to 37½p.

STRATEGY

(a) To incorporate the compulsory service of petit fours at luncheon and dinner.

(b) To advertise pre-theatre dinners at West End cinemas and theatres. To promote the restaurant within the theatres on the backs of theatre tickets, in programmes, etc.

(c) To build a small liqueur and coffee bar/lounge to stimulate a faster movement through the room.

REASONS FOR RECOMMENDATIONS

The achievement of any one of the objectives above should result in added net profitability before advertising costs in the region of £5 000–£7 650 per annum.

BUDGET RECOMMENDATION

The current appropriation of £1 000 per annum should be increased to £1 600 p.a. An amount of £1 000 should be appropriated to the continuance of the previous years' programmes. The additional amount of £600 should be expended as follows:

Item of expenditure	*Amount* (£)	
Brochures to be left at theatres	200	
Ticket advertising	150	
Programme advertising	150	
Entertaining	100	
	———	
	£600	
Sales estimates		
Additional diners	5 100	
Income per diner	1·50	
Cost of advertising, per new diner		12p
Total forecast net profit	15 000	
Total forecast net sales	100 000	
Cost of advertising per diner		3p
Profit: *15% of Sales*		
Last year		
Net profit	10 000	
Net sales	80 325	
Cost of advertising, per diner		2p
Profit: *12½% of Sales*		

ITEMISED BUDGET

This part of the plan should be devoted to the amount of itemised expenditure budgeted for each theatre, cinema, etc. The corresponding dates when it would be expended should also be incorporated.

COMPARISON WITH PREVIOUS BUDGETS

This is a comparison of the forecast expenditure with that of the previous year, showing the differences and reasons for such differences.

STATEMENT OF STRATEGY

This statement should have several copies, as it should be circulated as a guide to designers, the advertising department or agency. It should include the following guides:

(a) *Major objectives*. Statement of creative objectives.
(b) *Product*. Essential qualities, or characteristics, which should be reflected in the public's impression or image of the operation.
(c) *Sales appeals*. The most important competitive points.

MEDIA STRATEGY

The purpose of this statement is to define the methods of promotion, such as brochures, fire curtain slides, programmes, etc. Also included in the media strategy are media objectives, determining that area of the public to be reached and the timing and location of the operation.

SUPPORTING DATA

These should include any basic information pertinent to the report.

RECOMMENDATIONS

This should give a brief summary of:

(*a*) Promotional strategy.

(*b*) Budget recommendations.

(*c*) Copy strategy.

(*d*) Media strategy.

(*e*) Sales promotion policy.

APPENDIX

The appendix should include such items as:

(*a*) Sales estimates.

(*b*) Production problems (re petit fours in this example).

(*c*) Media plan.

(*d*) Description of copy and layout.

(*e*) The market (the theatre dinner market).

(*f*) Times of theatre meals.

(*g*) Competitive advertising.

(*h*) Competitive merchandising.

This chapter has dealt so far with the broad aspects of promotion and the compilation of a promotional plan. The component media used are discussed below.

TYPES OF ADVERTISING

Co-operative advertising and promotion

The British hotel industry has three co-operative marketing groups, namely, Prestige Hotels, Interchange Hotels and Historic Hotels of England.

Each is an informal association of hotels which have combined together to share marketing costs and compile marketing strategy. To date, they have been extremely successful. In fact, it is interesting to note that, although still only a few years old, they have had greater success in attracting tourists than many hotel groups.

National advertising

National advertising is undertaken by the British Travel Association overseas. However, so far no body has accepted the function of nationally advertising British restaurants, as is the case for other products.

Trade (wholesale) advertising

This type of advertising is becoming more important to the hotel industry, especially since it has adopted more sophisticated marketing and selling methods. Examples of wholesalers to whom operators could promote their businesses are coach operators, package tour operators and travel agents. Obviously, these 'middle men' are of great value to the industry and it is surprising how few caterers have exploited these markets.

Media

NEWSPAPERS AND MAGAZINES

National and local trade magazines and newspapers are the most popular form of catering advertising, and certainly cover the widest market for least cost. Nevertheless, it is doubtful whether, in most cases, the income derived justifies the cost involved. The professionally produced advertisements achieve the greater success, but they are comparatively few. Generally, there is a mediocre response to amateur advertising.

Because of the amount of wordage appearing in magazines and newspapers, it is essential that advertisements should stand out and be attractive to the reader. This is especially important in view of the habit of batching advertisements for similar products together.

OUTDOOR ADVERTISING

Outdoor advertising consists of posters or signs located in strategic positions along roads, on railway tracks and in cities. This is particularly important to motels, restaurants and other businesses which depend upon transient visitors. The message must be grasped easily and quickly, especially if traffic is travelling past at 60–70 m.p.h. Many operations ignore the fundamental fact that traffic travelling at high speeds must have adequate warning to enable it to stop. This medium would include car cards (posters in buses and trains) which, unlike posters, must have a point of intense interest to hold the reader's concentration over the available viewing period. A good example of this is the famous wool car cards.

DIRECT MAIL

This method of advertising is probably the most expensive form to carry out well. However, it has the advantage that the advertiser can control the market selection. Many novel forms of direct mail are in use and caterers interested in this form of promotion should visit the Direct Mail Exhibition which is held in London annually. A number of examples of high-response, direct mail shots are shown in the *Direct Mail Users Handbook*, a large proportion of which have received as high as 90% response. Direct mail is a valuable tool in the right hands and has been relatively unexploited in the British hotel and catering industry, although there are a few notable exceptions.

BUSINESS PUBLICATIONS

There are three types of business publication:

(a) Trade press for a particular industry.
(b) Management magazines.
(c) Professional journals.

The points to note are those which have already been described under newspapers and magazines above.

BROADCASTING

This medium has not been accepted readily by British caterers, basically because of the cost involved against the possible gain.

FILMS

Many caterers have slides or short films shown in cinemas and theatres which is, certainly, an improved selling approach to advertising in newspapers. However, from a marketing aspect it is doubtful whether cinema and theatre advertising is capable of the market coverage which newspapers obtain. It must also be remembered that fashion changes very rapidly. And, the composition of cinema and theatre audiences has altered greatly during the last decade.

CATALOGUES AND GUIDES

In the past ten years there has been a large increase in the number of catalogues and guides produced. But it is generally felt that the proportion which achieves any measurable effect is low. There are, however, one or two notable exceptions which have a good reputation both at home and overseas.

THE CATERER AND ADVERTISING

Usually, caterers consider large expenditure to be unnecessary for promoting their businesses and one is often asked what is a reasonable figure for advertising. The most acceptable range seems to be between 1·5 and 2·0%, which is a large enough budget to create impact and not so large that the company cannot afford it.

The role of advertising has five aims and it is doubtful whether the current ranges of promotional expenditure are planned or allocated in the best way to achieve them.

Combating competitive claims

Careful thought must be given to the impact gained by competitors and the strategy evolved to offset it. For this reason it is important that the caterer is well aware of his competitors' promotional efforts as well as their products.

Making potential customers aware of the product

The caterer must be certain that all of the potential market is aware of his operation. Previous chapters have described how small a restaurant market can be, and it is, therefore, absolutely essential that everyone is aware not only of the operation, but of the image it wishes to portray.

Persuading people to visit the operation

Advertising must be attractive enough to the potential customer to motivate him to visit the operation. Naturally, this means that the media, copy and layout must project a uniqueness and novelty which will encourage the customer to make a choice favouring the operation.

Inducing prospective customers to ask for further literature or request a visit from a salesman

The promotional material will isolate the needs of the potential market so that customers will wish to contact the operation to find out more about how these needs may be discharged—this aim is particularly pertinent to the sale of conference and banqueting facilities.

Reminding customers to buy

Advertising should also be used as a reminder to existing customers, to encourage frequent repeat business.

ADVERTISING TECHNIQUES RELEVANT TO THE CATERING INDUSTRY

Several techniques have been evolved by advertising men based on their knowledge of the market and how to influence it.

Basic appeals

The most successful advertisements have been based upon appeals to universal human likes and dislikes. The advertiser attracts the prospect's attention and proves to him that the advertised product can satisfy a basic need. 'Attention-getters' are: provocative headlines; striking photographs; catchy music; and the word 'free'. The simpler the device, the better.

Confidence builders

Advertisements must be convincing. People have to believe what is said before they will buy the product. Advertising devices which build confidence are: realistic photographs; testimonials; 'before' and 'after' pictures; clear and simple copy.

The 'you' angle

Everyone is interested in himself. Therefore, one technique of advertising is to tell the individual what the product will do for him— relevant to romantic restaurants, prestige conferences and banqueting suites. This may be projected by pictures of someone enjoying himself with whom the customer can identify himself, or by using the imperative 'See you at *André's*'.

Immediate sale

There are a number of methods for convincing a customer to act immediately. 'Come tonight' forms a simple device of urgency. A cut price suggests immediate action as does 'Limited number of tables available'.

Good copy

Copywriting must enable the customer to taste, feel and assess, in advance of buying, whatever is offered for sale. One brilliant example of this was the Centre Hotels advertisement picturing the console of their new digital reservation computer with the headline: 'I've just taken over Centre Hotels'. The advertisement goes on to list the reasons why Centre Hotels are the reasonably priced popular hotel group that they are, with the accent on modernity of business methods and techniques.

Ease of perception

The advertisement must be easy to understand. The average person cannot spend much time on a commercial message which is not easy to grasp. House styles and slogans are used for memory association with the product and make it easy to remember. Examples of these are: 'Same good care everywhere'; 'Go where the action is'; 'Comfort and value'; and 'The grand manner'.

Choice of media

The selection of media to reach the right people at the right time is difficult because media are so diverse and specialised. The bases on which media will be selected are as follows:

(a) Quantity and quality of circulation of population.
(b) Type of population by age and income levels and taste.
(c) Occupation.
(d) Cost of space and time.

As can be seen from the above, advertising is an expensive business and a complicated one. Caterers are advised to check on their current expenditure and the effectiveness of the advertising, and to decide whether it could be aided by the selective use of professional advice.

REPRESENTATION

Because personal selling has become very popular during recent years in the hotel and catering industry, it justifies a short section in this chapter. It is almost certain that more hotels and restaurants will form co-operatives and employ certain specialists, one of whom will certainly be a salesman.

First, the sales team must be aware of every other promotional device used by the company, and also of promotional objectives and strategy, so that they can bring about their attainment. Further, the work must be orientated in the right area. Many catering salesmen have sold large contracts for accommodation and food sales at a lower price than the hotel's manager could have obtained. This has occurred because the salesman was not aware of the advertising plan, if indeed there was one, and consequently wasted his employer's time and money. The salesman must also determine sales quotes and territories compatible with the advertising plan, so that lists of calls may be built up and planned in accordance with promotional requirements.

It is a matter of policy whether salesmen call by appointment or indulge in 'cold calling'. Most companies are used to both methods. However, it has been found that cold calling is the least successful of the two, although making appointments involves a considerable amount of office work.

It is important that salesmen are adequately equipped with promotional material orientated to this particular method of selling. All too often salesmen are sent out with a few hotel brochures rather than with material relevant to what has to be sold, e.g. banqueting, entertaining, parties, etc. There is no doubt that personal selling in catering has largely contributed to the ability of some establishments to force their sales far above breakeven point and, therefore, to enjoy substantially greater rates of profit than hitherto.

11
Purchasing wine

Wine, like any other product which a company sells, requires complete understanding of its characteristics before it can be sold effectively, i.e. in any worthwhile volume. The restaurant manager or sommelier who has reasonable knowledge about the wine he has to sell will be better able to persuade the customer to buy wine and to enjoy what he buys. In addition, a few words about the wine's origin and character will increase the customer's enjoyment.

Most food and beverage managers acquire a vast knowledge of food service and control and very little of the *beverage* side of the business. One has merely to consider the imbalance of the two products in terms of knowledge of marketability to realise this. Because the range of wine (one is excluding the multitude of lesser known wines) is, in fact, fairly limited, there is little excuse for the aspiring food and beverage manager not to acquire the necessary knowledge. This can be done by reading some of the books written by well-known wine experts and by attending wine tastings. Courses are organised by certain wine merchants and by the Guild of Sommeliers.

The most important part of the food and beverage manager's job in relation to wine is, obviously, to select a suitable list for the operations which he administers. The wine list, as much as the menu and the design, must constitute a continuation of the marketing needs of the operation. For example, at one extreme is the cheap and cheerful, fast-service bistro where red, white and rosé wines out of mock wooden barrels satisfy the markets, whilst at the other is the very gastronomic 'haute cuisine' establishment, requiring to please a connoisseur clientele. Of course, most operations fall between the two extremes, but whilst deciding the type of wine in accordance with the class of establishment, it must not be forgotten that there are 'fun' wines as well, which could suit either speciality or 'fun' establishments. Examples are Retsina, Moroccan, Portuguese and various Italian wines.

STOCKING THE CELLAR

The wine list must also, of course, suit the size of pocket and storage space available to the establishment. The dangers of overstocking have been amplified in other chapters but are worth repeating here. A recent trend has been to buy wine in bulk from the Continent but this has proved to be a risky occupation. Also, there are very few operations which can afford to lay down wines in view of the return they must certainly require from capital invested. This must be at least 11% at today's interest rates.

It is dangerous to attempt to lay down wines for lengthy periods of time. For example, there is one very famous club in New York where members lay down valuable wines for special occasions. One could, for instance, do this for one's son's 21st birthday on the day of his birth. Quite what would happen at the great occasion one cannot be sure, as the oppressive heat of the cellar would turn the wines sour in the first few months. It would be a much better strategy to have one's merchant keep the wine in his cellars and to pay for them as they are required, rather than take the risks of allowing an expensive cellarful of vinegar to depreciate at 10% per annum.

Purchasing stocks as and when they are required

This is done on a monthly basis and is the way in which most wine merchants would like to operate. But, in general, catering cash flows do not allow such short terms of credit and caterers are obliged to consider other methods of supply.

Sale or return

Most reputable merchants offer this facility and will change the stock left at the end of one year for wines on the new year's list, crediting the caterer with the returned wines at full cost price.

Lengthy credit terms

These are offered by some merchants to obtain business, the terms normally being three months. This has obvious advantages for the caterer but tends to obscure the real position which might well be a very large, current creditor state; it must also not be forgotten that the merchant is not giving credit for nothing and will charge somewhere along the line.

EXAMPLE

If the merchant reckons on a 12% return he will not allow the caterer to consume interest on capital at the rate of, e.g., 10% without building it into the price. Of course, although one may be prepared for this, the effect will be as follows:

Month	Value of wine delivered, £
1	3 000
2	4 000
3	3 000

Month 1 would be paid for in month 4, which would mean a loss of return to the merchant of approximately 10% on capital:

$$\frac{10}{100} \times \frac{3}{12} \times £3\,000 = £75$$

The caterer may well accept an increased cost of $2\frac{1}{2}\%$ for his credit facility. But there are not many who would be willing to write off $1\frac{1}{4}\%$ of sales, which is what it amounts to.

This credit system used to be a popular way for merchants to get into new operations, as the caterer in a time of high expense had only to pay for what he had sold. This, in effect, is similar to the three-month credit arrangement with the same disadvantages.

The other factor which affects purchasing policy is the adequacy of cellar storage space. This determines the frequency of delivery which may be from fortnightly or weekly to almost daily. Although infrequent deliveries require careful stock appraisal to ensure that stocks are not built up excessively, it must be remembered that most red wines of good quality require at least two weeks to settle. In any event, it is essential that stockholdings are controlled by a 'mini-max' system, or that buying is geared to par stocks.

CATEGORIES OF WINE

Whatever the method of purchase, the food and beverage manager must be able to select a well-balanced list and must have a clear idea of the main wine categories to be included in the sales strategy. The list should offer a reasonable selection from the main wine-producing areas in Europe, e.g. Bordeaux, Burgundy, Champagne, the Loire, the Rhône Valley and Moselle. 'Funny' wines from little-known regions will only sell if they are built up as 'house specialities,' which in itself is a good idea.

Basically, wine may be categorised into three main types. These are carafe wines, generic and 'little' wines and, lastly, what one expert calls 'swagger' wines.

Cheap and cheerful carafe wines

These are called 'house wines' and have no generic antecedents. For wine in this category the only factor to be considered is whether or not it is good drinking in relation to its price.

Generic and 'little' wines

These originate from small vineyards and it is regarding this type of wine that suspicions have been raised concerning its supply to the British market, in the past few years. The wines, blended and sweetened, frequently appeared under such names as 'Nuits St. Georges' or 'Volnay' rather than a brand name.

A rapid growth in the consumption of wine in this country encouraged this form of practice; however, the control of misrepresentation by statute and Britain's membership of the Common Market assured both restaurateur and the public alike that his wine is what it says on the label. Britain's entry into the Common Market necessitates that all merchants obey the *Appellation Contrôlée* laws and buy wines with an *'acquit vert'*.

Honesty is the best policy in the sale of wine. It is much more sensible to buy a wine such as Bourgogne Rouge and sell it as *'Une bonne bouteille'*, with a description of the wine, than to sell it under its brand name. Wines such as these may be obtained very reasonably, if London bottled.

'Swagger' wines

These wines are declared vintage and estate bottled. They are generally expensive and tend to appear on British wine lists as smart decoration—there being one bottle in the dispense bar and one in the bin. They can range from, for example, wines from the Upper Loire to first-growth clarets and wines from the Domaine de la Romanée Conti, and are sold at high prices. A sub-division of this category are bin-ends bought at wine auctions, often of considerable age. They are a gamble to buy but are sometimes very profitable. However, they normally require decanting in advance, which may throw a strain on the service.

SERVICE

The degree of service depends largely on the types of wine one sells. However, whatever the wine, it should be given the normal care and attention that any wine deserves, including being served at the correct temperature. The much-discussed question of cradle *versus* standing bottle is not important, although one could say that a cradle is less likely to be knocked over and the bottle is less agitated in pouring. However, the time spent on the table is not likely to make much difference to settling wine which has been badly shaken up.

The more expensive the wine, the more pretentious the service and this should be the case when one considers how much the customer is paying for it. The question of service is one which can easily be organised but the ability of the sommelier to advise his customer and display his knowledge is not so easy to develop. For example, if one buys 'Chateau Lafite' for the first time, one expects to find out rather more about it than just the fact that it is red. Also, the origin of cheaper wines can be interesting, e.g. 'Entre Deux Mers' is an unusual name and the customer would probably like to know about it.

The wine list should not be regarded as the ultimate in sales aids, but merely a well-designed price list. It should be supported by sommeliers who can expand on the brief notes of the list and are allowed to demonstrate their ability as salesmen. A cheap, easy-to-read, very helpful little book is *A Bluffer's Guide to Wine*, written by N. Clarke and published by Wolfe.

As has been mentioned previously, knowledge of wine is best gained from training sessions and wine merchants should be able to organise these, as it is in their interests, as well as the caterers', that wine sales should increase.

THE COMPOSITION AND DESIGN OF THE WINE LIST

The composition of the list is, obviously, an important exercise in that the complete range of wine products must be a reflection of the meal experience and the market mood of the restaurant.

Apart from very expensive restaurants, where wine selection should be a serious business, the list should be both amusing and informative. People eat out for entertainment and this need should be satisfied in both wine list and menu. The services of a copywriter should be utilised to ensure that the copy will be acceptable to a wide range of clientele.

Personal preference must be ignored and the customer's needs made paramount. The food and beverage manager may be a serious student of wine and, in that event, object to some of the increasing numbers of branded wines appearing on the list. But it may well be that a proportion of customers feel happier and more secure if they see a well-known wine on the list, such as 'Crown of Crowns'. For that reason it would be worth considering it. Constructing a wine list is like any other marketing exercise: sell what the customer wants not what one thinks he ought to have. The caterer is not a schoolteacher and should not endeavour to *educate* his customers.

Considerable stress has been laid upon the importance of the food and beverage manager's ability to produce a wine list which, in both content and typographical layout, is compatible with the meal experience provided. But it must also be remembered that an extension of this is the training of sommeliers to not only appreciate wine and its history but to utilise this knowledge in tactfully steering the customer to a wine which will give him satisfaction and value for money.

BRANDED WINES

In recent years many branded wines have come to the fore and more are being promoted every year. Such wines are 'Justine', 'Nicolas', 'Don Cortez', 'Blue Nun', 'Mateus Rosé', and 'Crown of Crowns', to mention a few.

Whilst it is admitted that the wines in question are disliked by most serious wine drinkers because they believe (and there is merit in the argument) that money spent on national advertising cannot also be put into a bottle, it is also true to say that such wines have materially contributed to the growing popularity of wine in this country.

Many people drinking wine for the first few occasions have only to visit three or four restaurants to become thoroughly confused with the seeming multitudes of brands available. The branded, nationally advertised wines provide a stable anchor for the customer who knows that such a wine will taste the same wherever he goes and he knows what he is paying for. Hopefully, this customer will move on to less well-known categories of wine, but, as in any new experience, he will start slowly and cautiously.

There is no doubt that the branded wines have introduced the public at large to the enjoyment of wine, and for that reason the catering industry should be duly grateful for the increase in volume of wine sales which has and will continue to be enjoyed.

12

Bar and cellar stockholding

The storage of wines, ales, spirits and minerals is a subject which has been covered in a number of catering textbooks. The question of physical storage has been fully dealt with in these publications and has also been briefly discussed in Chapter 8. Therefore, only basic points are reproduced here. However, the control of stock through adequate and meaningful records is one aspect which is often omitted and, consequently, is described at some length in this chapter.

PHYSICAL STORAGE

Cleanliness

A cellar should always be kept clean. Bottles covered with dust may look very well in the cellar, but labels ingrained with dirt do not look so attractive on the table. Also, grease and dirt on floors increase the danger of slipping with heavy loads.

Stock held

Stock held should always err on the low side for two main reasons:

(a) The interest charges which have to be paid on cash locked up in stock.

(b) The risk of stock ageing if it is not turned around properly. Even when reducing stock to minimum levels, one should remember that red wines take at least a fortnight to settle after delivery.

Rotation

The stock should be rotated on a strict first-in, first-out basis (FIFO). This will ensure that none is pushed to the back of the shelves or a crate left at the bottom, allowing the contents to become undrinkable.

Temperature

When storing liquor it is essential that a 'steady' temperature be maintained. This should be approximately 56–60°F to prevent cask beer and some spirits from deteriorating.

Delivery

When stock is delivered it should be unwrapped and taken out of the cartons. In any event, stock levels should be sufficiently low to obviate any need for storing bottles in cartons.

Racking

In most operations wines are laid horizontally in racks, either in specially constructed bins or in boxes which are as good and are not quite so expensive (*Figure 12.1*). Boxed racking is easier for

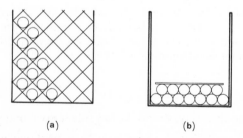

(a)   (b)

Figure 12.1. Two types of wine racking: (a) special; (b) boxed

stocktaking purposes if splints are placed between each row, which should contain a uniform number of bottles. Spirits and liqueurs should be stored vertically on shelves. Again the rows should contain uniform numbers of unwrapped bottles.

Stocktaking checklists should conform with the cellar racking order to shorten the time of stock checking, and to ensure that items are not overlooked.

Bar storage

The amount of stock held in a bar should be governed directly by the sales volume of those items. A convenient measure is to use the equivalent of three-sevenths of a week's sales at cost. Apart from

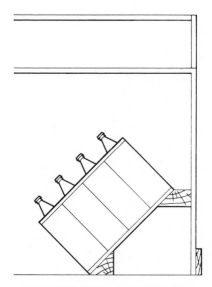

Figure 12.2. Method of storing beer

easier stock checking and control, it is sensible to minimise liquor stocks in places where temperatures change radically from one part of the day to another.

Sales items should be situated in places which are near to hand in relation to their popularity. Obviously, popular spirits will be placed on wall optics directly behind the barman. Because baby minerals are the most often served items in any bar, they should be shelved under the spirit optics. A useful method of storing beers, which has been adopted by some establishments, is to keep them crated beneath the bar top to save having to remove them from the crates (*Figure 12.2*).

Bar design

The object of stocking a bar is to equate the least amount of stock with the maximum sales and maximum convenience to those working the bar. Back bar fittings are a frequent source of annoyance to bartenders, having been planned more as an intricate jigsaw puzzle

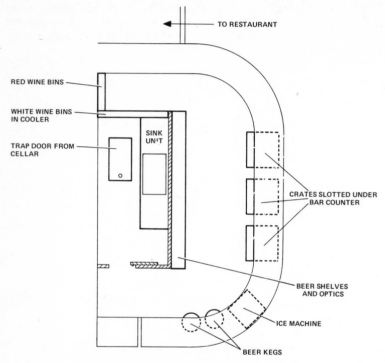

Figure 12.3. Example of bar layout

rather than as a service aid. Although this chapter is not concerned with bar design, the convenience of bar service and storage is important.

The bar illustrated in *Figure 12.3* is not perfect, but does include interesting features, some of which are described below.

CURVED COUNTER

A curved bar counter allows greatest coverage with the minimum amount of movement. An ice-making machine fits flush with the counter and, also, kegs and crates can be slotted into it.

BACK ROOM

The back fitting encloses a small room which is unusual for most bars in this country. It allows someone to be employed part time for washing glasses, thus obviating any need to utilise a good barman for this job in busy periods. The room can also be used for extra storage, if necessary. A feature of this room is that it contains a trapdoor, allowing a hoist to be used to deliver liquor and remove empties.

STOCKHOLDING

Bar and cellar stocks should be held on a par basis, i.e. a minimum stock should be assessed from which staff should not deviate. This should be based upon three days' sales, bearing in mind that requisitions may be made daily.

Normally, bars will not require to hold more than three bottles of the house spirits and one bottle of each of the others. Nor should it require to hold more than one bottle of liqueur, and, in most cases, liqueurs may be restricted to a few popular brands. Minerals should be carefully considered, because they are delivered in batches of six dozen. This does not mean that bars should stock each variety in six dozens. This also, of course, applies to beers.

The par stock for each item should be established and recorded. This record will be incorporated in the stock control system discussed in Chapter 18. The amounts of stock held in the cellar will be based upon bar and function requirements, in conjunction with minimum orderable quantities and delivery dates. A tolerance will normally be built in to safeguard against accidents and emergencies. The calculation for assessing par stockholding is as follows:

Item—Purple Horse Whisky

Average summer* consumption (26 weeks)	270 bottles
Average weekly consumption	10 bottles
Order to delivery time	14 days
This is equivalent to 2 weeks' consumption	20 bottles
Add tolerance	4 bottles
Par cellar stock	24 bottles
Minimum orderable quantity	24 bottles

* Par stocks will normally be different for summer and winter.

Marked bottles

The stock control system advocated here incorporates the marking of bottles by the cellarman. It is recommended that a signature stamp is used which cannot be easily copied and that stamping is a strict part of the cellarman's routine.

Bottle-for-bottle issues

The system also includes the utilisation of bottle-for-bottle issues, whereby no bottle is issued without receiving a properly marked empty in return. Obviously, circumstances will prevent caterers from exercising this rule on all occasions. However, the following general points should be adhered to:

(a) Individual bar stock bottles, such as liqueurs, will be further requisitioned when the original is reduced to four-tenths.

(b) Minerals and beers will normally be exchanged in round dozens.

(c) House spirits and sherries, etc., will normally only be exchanged on a bottle-for-bottle basis.

The exchanged empties will be destroyed, usually by smashing. However, in situations where this is not possible, slicing through the label with a paper-knife has been found to be an adequate alternative.

BAR AND CELLAR RECORDS

Goods inwards book

The cellarman or goods inwards clerk will normally keep a goods inwards book for liquor deliveries. An example of a goods inwards book is shown in *Figure 12.4* and contains entries for the date of

Date	Supplier's name	Ales	Minerals	Liqueurs	Spirits	Wines	Total

Figure 12.4. Goods inwards book form

delivery, supplier's name, and value of goods. This type of goods inwards book is of value only where stock valuations are undertaken in cellar and bars, to provide the value of consumption. For example:

	£
Stock at start	1 200
Add goods inwards	4 000
Total	5 200
Less *Stock at start*	1 000
Cost of stock sold	£4 200

Obviously, most operations prefer additional internal controls, therefore they will wish to use a goods inwards book whose information may be utilised to furnish detailed information for internal records, as shown in *Figure 12.5*. The purpose of a goods inwards book

Date: 1.11.72	Food	Liquor	Maintenance	etc.
J. Bloggs	£499·92			
P. Jones		£98·81		

Figure 12.5. Detailed goods inwards book form

is to provide a record which may be adjusted for stocks to give costs so that they can be set against sales. It is also used to assess creditors at the end of the year for annual accounts.

Cellar inwards book

The cellarman will then record the items in detail in his own cellar inwards book (*Figure 12.6*). This book provides posting data for the

Date	Items	Bin No.	Bottles	Halves	Other sizes
4.2.69	Guinness	204	144	72	—
	Green Shield	218	96	48	—
	Bass	216	144	72	—
	Britannia	103	—	—	30 gal

Figure 12.6. Cellar inwards book form

cellarman's bin cards if they are kept, and also for the master
liquor stock ledger (see Chapter 18).

Invoices or delivery notes dealt with by the goods receiving clerk
or cellarman will be stamped and the relevant section completed.

Requisition forms

Liquor requisition forms will be completed by all departments
requiring liquor. These may be as follows:

(a) Bars.

(b) Kitchen.

(c) Night porter.

(d) Housekeeper (in those hotels where sherry is left in guests'
     rooms when they arrive).

Each of these departments will have a numbered duplicate requisition book used to record orders from the cellar. The requisitioned
items will be only those necessary to bring stock back to par. The
requisitions will be sent to the cellar, where the cellarman will make
up orders and sign the requisition to this effect. When the cellarman
delivers the order to the bar he will obtain the barman's signature
on the requisition as proof of delivery. The requisition will then be
sent to control for posting to the master liquor ledger.

The cellarman will also keep a record of ullages, breakages and
returns, which will be needed by the control department to adjust
the accounts and stocktaking reports.

Bar records

The barman is required to keep certain records to account for the
various transactions which occur in the bar. The easiest way to
consider this is illustrated in *Figure 12.7*.

CASH

Bar cash should be rung up on a cash register, preferably a machine
with a built-in audit roll on which every transaction is printed.
Normal cash balancing procedures will take place nightly, the till
being balanced against the audit roll total. A bar book is normally
kept in which the two totals are recorded, the difference being
observed daily.

OFF-SALES CASH

The difference between retail and off-sales value is normally re-corded in a book or on a check pad. The use of price differentials provides a loophole for a dishonest barman, who can sell a bottle

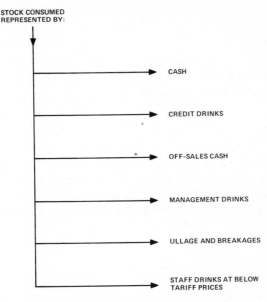

Figure 12.7. Bar stock consumption breakdown

through the optic for £4·80 and record it as an off-sale for £3, thus pocketing £1·80. Two methods of preventing this are as follows:

(a) Management should sign the off-sales record when an off-sale is made. As off-sales are comparatively rare this is normally not a hardship.

(b) Off-sales of specific items only should be sold, e.g. specific gins and whiskies. The off-sales will be $26\frac{2}{3}$ oz. bottles, whilst the bottles used on optic will all be 40 oz.

CREDIT DRINKS

Drinks sold to customers on credit will be recorded on a check pad or check machine. The checks so produced will be charged to customers' accounts through the establishment's sales accounting procedure.

MANAGEMENT DRINKS

Management drinks should be dealt with in exactly the same way as credit drinks, particularly with regard to signing before the end of the session when management can remember their precise order.

ULLAGE AND BREAKAGES

Beer used for cleaning, ullaged bottles and breakages will be recorded so that, where possible, a credit may be obtained from the supplier, and adjustments may be made to control records.

STAFF DRINKS

Staff drinks served at 'cost plus' prices pose a problem to caterers and require strict control. The easiest procedure to deal with this is to nominate a member of staff to write out the drinks order, which may be subsequently priced and adjusted in the stocktaking records.

13

The economics of food and beverage operations

CASH FLOW

The economics of any business operation can best be considered in terms of its cash flow, which is the speed at which cash flows in and out of the operation. Although profit and loss accounts are important, the real purpose beyond the generation of profit is the accrual of sums of cash for expansion or to reward the operator.

The fact that profit does not necessarily equal cash surplus, and that, in some cases, organisations enjoy profit and a cash deficit in the same year, is not easily understood by many non-accounting people. For these reasons, it is essential to control cash flows in and out of an operation.

The economics of food and beverage operations, therefore, involves two basic concepts. These are profit and cost levels and turn-round of cash.

EXAMPLE

If an operator purchases 10 lb of fillet steak at 75p per lb, he will incur an expenditure of £7·50 on one week's credit. If in the same week he sells 5 lb of the steak for £2·50 per lb, of which he takes £2·50 in cash, the balance being credit accounts, then the result is as follows:

Profit and loss	£	Cash flow	£
Purchases	7·50		
Less stock	3·75		
Consumption	3·75		
Sales	12·50	Cash sale	2·50
Gross profit	8·75	Cash in hand	2·50

The caterer, therefore, has made a gross profit of £8·75 but has at the same time cash only of £2·50. Should he continue to trade at this rate he will incur bank interest charges. If this is at 10%, the deficit will be increased by 10% per annum. In addition, wages and overheads must be paid, notwithstanding any deficit of cash temporarily suffered. Ignoring this function of 'cash management' is often the source of many of the predicaments of hotel and catering organisations.

Most industrial companies evaluate future projects in terms of cash flow, so important do they regard the generation of cash. From this practice has evolved the technique of discounted cash flow which is now generally accepted as the most rational method of appraising new developments.

The cash flow of a business organisation is, therefore, important and cannot be controlled by profit and loss accounts. The way in which to optimise cash flow is to examine all those things which would be included therein, but would *not* be included in the profit and loss account. Such items are normally those shown as current assets and current liabilities in the balance sheet.

Current assets

Current assets include stock, debtors and prepayments, together with cash, bank balance and trade investments. They are normally shown in balance sheet groupings as follows:

	£
Cash at bank	4 180
Cash in hand	100
Stock	6 000
Debtors	10 000
Prepayments	3 000
Trade investment	1 000
Total current assets	£24 280

STOCK

Included here are items in stock for which no revenue is accruing. If the operation is financed by an overdraft costing in the region of 10% per annum, then stock is actually costing money while sitting in the stores or cellar. It is important to operate at the lowest stock levels possible, because stock held merely ties up available cash which could be used for other purposes. Many caterers tend to over-stock at certain times to take advantage of reduced prices. This is quite acceptable provided that the saving exceeds bank rate and also that there will be cash available when payment is due. Stocks should be controlled at minimum levels at all points of storage, i.e. cellar, stores, bars, kitchen, etc. The methods of so doing are shown in following chapters.

DEBTORS

Many companies (especially caterers) allow debts to accumulate as they are afraid of losing goodwill. However, it should be realised that it is not worth while to conduct business with bad payers. Most caterers yield very low returns on sales; from 6% to 15% is normal. Consequently, a debt of 6 months' standing at 10% interest reduces profit by 5% immediately, as the caterers must finance it. It is good policy, therefore, to control debtors rigidly on a routine system, which should not have a cycle exceeding three months from the date of incurring the debt to enforced collection.

PREPAYMENTS

These are accounts normally paid in advance, e.g. subscriptions, rates, insurances, etc. It is surprising how these items can accumulate over a short period and they should be watched carefully. Where it is possible to take advantage of shorter payment periods, one should do so.

Current liabilities

Current liabilities consist of items which are payable in the short term, such as trade creditors, accrued items like electricity, gas and interest charges, short term loans and bank overdrafts.

TRADE CREDITORS

Many companies attempt to use their suppliers for finance by extracting as much as three months' credit from them. Apart from the fact that this causes ill feeling, especially if the suppliers are small, an economic crisis can result in considerable difficulties, with suppliers having to enforce shorter credit periods. In addition, it is extremely imprudent for any businessman to allow debts to reach such proportions that they cannot normally be covered without drastic action in the event of an emergency. Large credit periods may appear attractive as a cash conservation measure. However, the disadvantage of being at *risk* as well as having little come-back to suppliers of inferior goods at high prices, outweighs this considerably.

If a company adds an extension or a new unit to its existing operation, it may find itself short of working capital because underestimates of cash-raising requirements have obliged it to use current cash at bank to provide the balance. It is hoped that the new facilities will generate sufficient profit to enable the operation to extract itself from this position. However, this rarely happens and the result is often a permanent state of shortage or capital. Long credit periods, due to circumstances other than capital expenditure, generally indicate that the operation is either non-viable or badly managed (in the business sense) and a thorough investigation should take place.

ACCRUALS

Accruals are normally quarterly or bi-annual items such as electricity and interest charges, and often tend to be forgotten or ignored. When the amount of the bill is known it can provide quite a shock, unless a clear indication of what it might be is known, by recording meter readings and calculation of interest owing, etc., month by month.

SHORT-TERM LOANS AND BANK OVERDRAFT

In the last few years especially, companies having to reduce short-term loans or bank overdrafts have been badly hit. This has been further aggravated if these items were regarded as permanent working capital.

Correlation of current assets and current liabilities

Although accountants total current assets and current liabilities and show the difference as either surplus or deficit of working capital, the exercise is rarely meaningful.

EXAMPLE

The figures opposite show a surplus of working capital of £160. However, should creditors' payments and accruals (£8 000) be reduced from three months' credit to one (as happened in spring 1969) then the sum of £5 333 plus £900 tax liability must be found— a total of £6 233. Cash at bank equals £2 000 and a little could be obtained from the remaining items such as debtors and stock. Therefore, a cash problem in the region of £3 500–£4 000 will be experienced. At the same time it should be noted that interest is being lost on excess debtors and stock to reduce cash in-flow continuously.

Current assets	£	£
Cash at bank	2 000	
Cash in hand	60	
Debtors	2 000	
Prepayments	1 000	
Stock	3 000	
Trade investments	1 000	9 060
Current liabilities		
Creditors	6 000	
Accruals	2 000	
Current taxation	900	8 900
Surplus of working capital		£160

There have been many books published which consider the points above in depth. For the purposes of this chapter, however, a simple example of a hotel balance sheet is given in *Figure 13.1* to indicate the areas most pertinent to caterers and hotelkeepers. From the balance sheet the following points may be noted:

THE RATIO OF FIXED ASSETS TO CURRENT ASSETS IS 23/67—1:3 APPROXIMATELY

The current assets are far in excess of normal requirements and must result in excess cash being tied up in the project with resultant heavy interest charges.

THE RATIO OF CURRENT ASSETS TO CURRENT LIABILITIES IS 11/23—1:2 APPROXIMATELY

The ratio is acceptable. However, a reduction of current assets will indicate a similar reduction of current liabilities to keep the two items to a safe relationship.

THE RATIO OF WORKING CAPITAL TO FIXED ASSETS IS 12/67—1:6
APPROXIMATELY

This ratio emphasises the surplus cash involved in the project. The ratio should be increased from 1:8 to 1:10 in order to allow surplus funds to be released.

Account	Fixed assets, £	Depreciation, £	Balance, £
Buildings	50 000	—	50 000
Furniture	10 000	4 000	6 000
Plant	15 000	5 000	10 000
Motor vehicles	2 000	500	1 500
Total	£77 000	* £9 500	£67 500
Current assets			
Cash at bank	7 000		
Cash in hand	200		
Debtors	5 000		
Prepayments	2 000		
Stock	8 000		
Trade investment	1 000	23 200	
Total	£23 200		
Current liabilities			
Trade creditors	6 000		
Accruals	1 000		
Short-term loan	3 000		
Current taxation	1 000	11 000	
			12 200
Total	£11 000		
Net assets			£79 700
Represented by:			
Share capital			50 000
Profit and loss account			9 700
Loans			20 000
			£79 700

Figure 13.1. Balance sheet — Blue Boar Hotel

THE RATIO OF STOCK TO PURCHASES IS 8/32—1:4

This indicates a stock turn-round of only four times annually, which should be increased to eight or nine times, thus releasing half the stock cash value.

THE RATIO OF DEBTORS TO SALES IS 5/80—1 :16

This indicates that debtors are worth 23 days' sales on average, which is too high for a mainly cash business and should be reduced to from 10 to 15 days' sales, i.e. by £1 500 to £2 700.

PREPAYMENTS

Prepayments are too high and should be reduced substantially by judicious examination of the items composing same, i.e. by £500 to £750.

CREDITORS

This represents two months' purchases and it is recommended that it be reduced to one month.

SHORT-TERM LOAN AT 12%

This loan should be discharged by cash at bank after reduction of current assets.

Effect of the above recommendations

Table 13.1 shows the effect of the above recommendations, which have served to illustrate the importance of a correct financial structure, together with the routine endeavour to conserve cash. A tool to help managements to undertake this is the forecast cash flow, which will indicate periods of cash shortage.

EXAMPLE

An example of a simple cash flow is shown overleaf. It must be remembered that the physical payment and income dates are important here, e.g. purchases for June's food production will not be paid until August or September. The cash flow only takes into account the fact that debtors may enjoy two or three months' credit.

Table 13.1 Results of recommendations on current assets and liabilities

Item	Before, £	Now, £	Difference, £
Current assets			
Cash at bank	7 000	5 000	2 000
Cash in hand	200	200	—
Debtors	5 000	2 500	2 500
Prepayments	2 000	1 400	600
Stock	8 000	4 000	4 000
Trade investment	1 000	—	1 000
Total	£23 200	£13 100	£10 100
Current liabilities			
Trade creditors	6 000	3 000	3 000
Accruals	1 000	1 000	—
Short-term loan	3 000	—	3 000
Current taxation	1 000	1 000	—
Total	£11 000	£5 000	£6 000
Release of cash			£4 100

			£
May 1st	*Balance at bank*		(2 300)
Cash sales	39 000		
March debtors	3 000		
	———	42 000	
less March invoices		31 000	
		11 000	
May salaries		9 000	2 000
June 1st	*Balance at bank*		(300)
Cash sales	38 000		
April debtors	2 000		
	———	40 000	
less April invoices		28 500	
		11 500	
June salaries		8 500	
		———	3 000
July 1st	*Balance at bank*		£2 700

Having discussed the effects of financial structure and cash conservation, one must consider this in the light of the profitability of food and beverages generally.

COST AND PROFIT LEVELS

There are three main items of expense, as shown in *Table 13.2*, and each item is dealt with separately. The profit of the operation is

Table 13.2 Cost and profit levels

Item	£	%
Sales	40 000	100
1. *Direct materials*	23 000	57
Gross margin	17 000	43
2. *Wages*	1 000	2·5
Net margin	16 000	40·5
3. *Distribution costs*	4 000	10
Balance	12 000	30·5

dependent upon these three levels and their interaction. Therefore, it is essential that the profit levels are correctly set in relation to the type of business envisaged.

Sales

In food and beverage operations *sales* are made up of the income accruing from food sales, liquor sales and other minor items such as gaming machines, hire of band, etc. For the purpose of this exercise only food and beverages will be considered.

It has become popular in hotel and catering operations to interpret all costs in terms of sales, i.e. sales equals 100% and costs are shown as a percentage of sales. It is this method which has been adopted in this book.

SALES MIX

When considering catering profitability, one must first consider the effect of sales mix. From the essentially similar operations shown in *Table 13.3*, both costing £50 000 to build, it can be seen that although A and B take the same amount in turnover, B is more profitable than A. Thus for *return on capital*, A: 24%; B: 26%. The reason for this result is that B sold more food than A, which accrues a higher gross profit than liquor.

Table 13.3 Effect of sales mix

Item	A £	A %	B £	B %
Sales				
Food	20 000		30 000	
Liquor	30 000		20 000	
Total	£50 000	100	£50 000	100
Costs				
Food	6 000	12	9 000	18
Liquor	12 000	24	8 000	16
Total	£18 000	36	£17 000	34
Gross margin	32 000	64	33 000	66
Wages	10 000	20	10 000	20
Net margin	22 000	44	23 000	46
Overheads	10 000	20	10 000	20
Balance	12 000	24	13 000	26

It must not be assumed that it is always desirable to sell more food than beverages; other cost items must also be considered. For example, the wages paid to dispense beverages may be lower than those paid to serve and prepare food. The whole operational concept, therefore, must be examined.

COST OF SALES

In a previous chapter, a range of food gross profit levels has been shown, indicating the difference between different types of catering operations. A varying range also applies to liquor and may differ from 40% to 70% dependent upon prices charged and product mix.

Food

The caterer must ensure that his menu, whether table d'hôte, à la carte, or permanent, should in total generate the gross margin he needs to make the operation profitable. The component dishes must be balanced so that high-priced dishes are adequately offset by low-priced dishes. Assuming that the menu has been planned to take this into account, then any variations from target gross margin will show as follows:

(a) *Usage variance.* Pilfering, over-portioning or wastage.

(b) *Price variance.* Under- or over-payment for raw materials.

(c) *Staff feeding variance.* Under- or over-provision for staff feeding.

(d) *Menu composition variance.* Indicates profit or loss gained from menu mix.

These variances are discussed in greater detail in Chapters 17, 18 and 19.

Liquor

Liquor gross profits will vary according to the amounts of the liquor items sold, all of which carry differing gross profit levels (*Table 13.4*). It is, therefore, important that the price structure of liquor

Table 13.4 Liquor gross profits

Item	Gross profit, %
Wines	50–60
Spirits	50–60
Ales	20–40
Minerals	30–60
Cigarettes	10–15

items reflects the market taste and, at the same time, generates the maximum gross profit from the operation.

Table 13.5 indicates a guide to liquor gross margins. Breweries operating tied houses should add their wholesale mark-up to the

Table 13.5 Liquor gross margins

Establishment	Gross margin, %
Top class international hotel	60–70
Haute cuisine restaurants and clubs	55–60
Good quality hotel (4 star)	50–53
Medium class hotel	45–50
Public houses (spirit bias)	35–45
Public houses (beer bias)	30–40

margins quoted. The list given in the table is not exhaustive and can only serve as a guide, as there are many differing types of hotel and restaurant operation.

The above margins apply only to the UK and *must not* be assumed for overseas. For example, liquor costs in some Mediterranean countries are one-quarter of the UK and many countries use different dispensing measures; for example, the Republic of Ireland has a standard measure of $\frac{1}{4}$ of a gill (20 out) as opposed to the UK measures of $\frac{1}{5}$ or $\frac{1}{6}$ of a gill.

Wages

It is clear that, because of sales mix and class of establishment, food and beverage operations do not make a standard rate of gross margin. Consequently, target gross margins differ from operation to operation. There will also be variations in rates of pay. For example, wages will differ according to the labour intensity of the operation. Where prepared foods are used, plate or self-service labour costs will be low, whilst haute cuisine silver service will be high.

Similarly, liquor wages differ according to the speed and mode of service. For example, a bar having waiter service will have a higher wage percentage cost than a bar with counter service because more staff are necessary and the waiters govern the rate of sales.

CONTROLLABLE OVERHEADS

The overheads of a food and beverage operation may be divided into two parts, as shown in *Table 13.6*, depending upon whether they are controllable or not. Although it is possible to make some minor adjustment to non-controllable items, e.g. rate appeals, cheaper insurance, decreased bank indebtedness, etc., they are not as flexible as the controllable items and are not normally affected by management action.

Table 13.6 Food and beverage overheads

Controllable	Non-controllable
Administrative	Depreciation
Advertising	Rents, rates and insurance
Heat, light, power	Audit fees, bank interest, etc.
General expenses	Maintenance

Administration

The cost of administration varies between one operation and another and is dependent upon the following factors:

(a)   Whether or not the operation belongs to a group.

(b)   Whether or not it is managed or owner-managed.

(c)   How much management control is evident.

Most well-informed managements are beginning to realise the value of the administrative function. No longer is it considered an expensive one which could be done without if necessary, but as a management tool to decrease overheads and increase sales. This is the industrial philosophy now creeping into catering. It demands high-calibre managements to control administration adequately in order to carry out the true function of management in attaining management objectives.

The cost of administration varies between 2% and 8% depending on the conditions under which the operation is run. Most operations carry an administrative cost of between 3% and 5%. It is certain that operations at peak efficiency will be obliged to spend up to 8% of their turnover to maintain optimum profitability and growth.

Advertising and promotion

There are very few operations which are household words and, therefore, do not spend large amounts on advertising. For the majority of operations, however, a well-planned promotional scheme is highly necessary. Promotional costs vary between 1% and 5% of turnover, depending on whether professional assistance is sought and also upon the media used.

General

This would include sundry items such as flowers and décor, etc., and would normally cost between 1% and 2% of turnover.

Heat, light, power

The cost of this item varies from 2·5% to 5·0% of turnover, depending on the age of the building, the tariffs agreed and the methods of saving power employed by the operation. It is essential that hotels and catering operations examine their power costs at intervals, preferably utilising the services of a consultant who may negotiate tariffs and recommend economic methods of operation.

Repairs and maintenance

This is one area of cost which is often disputed amongst hoteliers and caterers. The function of maintenance expenditure is two-fold:

(a) To maintain the operation as it was at its commencement.
(b) To keep abreast of new development in furnishings, décor and equipment so that they may be incorporated in the unit.

Many operations spend very little on maintenance. They, therefore, become old-fashioned and shabby within a few years. This is reflected in profit over the initial period, which is high, because little is being expended on maintenance. However, when lack of maintenance causes sales to fall the operation is unable to maintain its initial performance without considerable capital expenditure and disruption. Further, as new capital is taxed income, it will be considerably harder to find than maintenance charged annually *before taxation* from profits.

Inefficient operations frequently mask their low profitability because of a lack of maintenance expenditure and should examine their operations critically in the light of this.

Maintenance expenditure, including working replacements such as uniforms, linen, china, etc., is normally expected to range from 5 to 12% of turnover, depending upon age and quality of previous maintenance. The accounting system advocated here charges working replacements to food, liquor, etc., so that they may be controlled separately and the balance of maintenance at a rate of 5–7% to profits.

A *pro forma* accounts presentation for a food and beverage operation is shown in Chapter 20 (long form) while *Figures 13.2–13.4* show some examples of different types of operation.

For comparison purposes the examples are shown in the short form presentation, which differs from the long form as follows:

(a) Wages except for administration are charged in total in short form.
(b) All distributed costs normally chargeable to the food and liquor schedules in the long form are charged to *general* in the short form.

Item	£	%	
Sales			
Food	40 000	67	
Liquor	20 000	33	
	£60 000	100	
Cost of sales			
Food	12 000	30	À la carte only
Liquor	8 000	40	
	£20 000	33	
Gross margin	40 000	67	
Wages and staff costs	20 000	33	Includes SET, grad. pens., NHI and staff feeding
Net margin	£20 000	34	Profit after wages
Administration	4 800	8	Includes administrative salaries
Advertising	3 000	5	Total promotion cost
Heat, light and power	2 000	3	Cost of oil, electricity, gas, water
General	1 200	2	Includes renewals, e.g. plate, china, etc.
Total	£11 000	18	
Control level	£9 000	16	Before non-controllable overhead comparable with any other food operation
Rent, rates, insurance	1 000	1	
Depreciation	200	½	
Repairs and maintenance	2 400	4	At 4% of turnover
Other additions and deductions	400	½	Includes bank interest, audit fees, etc.
Total	£4 000	6	
Net profit	£5 000	10	

Figure 13.2. Haute cuisine restaurant accounts

BREAKEVEN ANALYSIS

The technique of breakeven analysis is very simple and easy to operate. However, it is relatively unknown to caterers, which is unfortunate in view of the information it conveys. The advantage of the technique is that it can convey the situation of an operation under varying conditions, whilst a projected trading account can indicate a situation under a single set of conditions only.

Item	£	%
Sales		
Food	40 000	67
Liquor	20 000	33
Total	£60 000	100
Cost of sales		
Food	14 000	35
Liquor	10 000	50
Total	£24 000	40
Gross margin	36 000	60
Wages, etc.	15 000	25
Net margin	£21 000	35
†Administration	3 000	5
†Advertising	1 500	2·5
†Heat, light and power	1 500	2·5
†General	2 000	3
†Total	£8 000	13
†Control level	£13 000	22
†Rent, rates, insurance	1 200	2
†Depreciation	2 000	3
†Repairs and maintenance	4 200	7
†Other additions	1 000	2
†Total	£8 400	14
Net profit	£4 600	8

Figure 13.3. Hotel food and beverage operation accounts *

*This example indicates that the opinion held by many hoteliers that hotels cannot produce profit from their food operation is a fallacy.

†These items have been apportioned from total hotel expenses on the basis of sales.

The object of the exercise is to graph changing costs and wages against rising sales and to consider the effect on profit, as shown in *Figure 13.5*. Wages and costs are graphed at the same point vertically as the sales they would be required to support. The method is to

Item	£	%
Sales	20 000	100
Cost of sales	8 000	40
Gross margin	£12 000	60
Wages, etc.	4 000	20
Net margin	£8 000	40
Expenses		
Administration	1 500	7·5
Advertising	200	1
Heat, light and power	1 000	5
General	1 000	5
Total	£3 700	18·5
Control level	£4 300	21·5
Fixed costs		
Rent, rates, insurance	1 000	5
Depreciation	200	1
Repairs and maintenance	400	2
Other additions	200	1
Total	£1 800	9
Net profit	£2 500	12·5

Figure 13.4. Self-service restaurant (food only) accounts

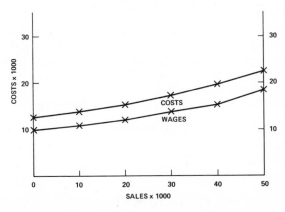

Figure 13.5. Breakeven analysis

consider four or five points on the sales axis (e.g. 10 000s) and consider the wages and overhead necessary to support it. A line would then be drawn through the points to indicate the trend. The gross profit line would then be drawn from the intersection of the axis as in *Figure 13.6*. The operation shown in our fictional break-even chart would break even at £30 000 sales and incur a very rapid rate of net profit thereafter. However, should the operation

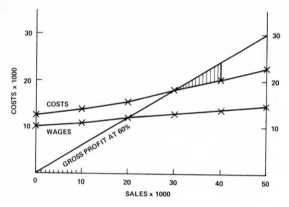

Figure 13.6. Final breakeven chart

not achieve 60% gross margin it is important to consider the effect on net profit, and breakeven and further gross margin lines may be superimposed upon the chart to indicate them.

INVESTMENT APPRAISAL

Many references are made to feasibility studies in the industry, but with little idea of what constitutes a feasibility study. It is an investment appraisal with one objective and that is to ascertain what return on capital one can expect from a project in order to decide whether or not to invest in it.

This involves several phases in the following sequence:

(*a*)   The discovery of, and definition of, business concept.

(*b*)   Market research.

(*c*)   Market assessment.

(*d*)   Financial feasibility.

These have all been considered in earlier chapters and in the case study of *Moonstone Restaurants* (pages 25–33).

It is at this stage that most caterers cannot decide whether the project is feasible or not. The financial forecast may indicate a profit, but does not show the results of the first two years of trading* or subsequent years to the first optimum year. This information is available from the breakeven chart. By estimating sales through the life of the project the profits for each year may be obtained.

In addition, it is important to calculate the cash flows in and out of the project and the profit accruing from those cash flows. The net cash flow may be estimated by adding back depreciation to profit and deducting tax payable, as shown in *Table 13.7*. It should be

Table 13.7 Net cash flow estimation

Year	Net profit, £	Deprecia- tion, £	Total, £	Tax at 45%, £	Net cash flow, £
1	(20 000)	5 000	(15 000)	—	(15 000)
2	50 000	5 000	55 000	—	55 000
3	60 000	5 000	65 000	18 000	48 000
4	62 000	5 000	67 000	29 250	37 750

noted that Year 1 shows a loss, therefore no tax is payable and is offset against tax payable in Year 2. Taxation is payable one year in arrears.

WHAT RETURN?

During 1969–70 capital became scarce and is likely to remain so for a number of years. This indicates that a return on capital of less than 20% before taxation (12% after taxation) is unrealistic. For investment appraisal purposes a return of 12% after taxation is used as the criterion return.

The final calculation is based upon the discounted cash flow technique of investment appraisal, which is explained in previous publications.†

---

* The above assumes that most operations do not enjoy optimum profitability until the third trading year.

† FEARN, D. A., *Management Systems for the Hotel, Catering and Allied Industries*, Business Books, London (1969); and *The Practice of General Management: An Hotel and Catering Application*, Macdonald, London (1971).

14
Kitchen planning

Most caterers who read this book will have worked in a kitchen at some time or another. Therefore, many of the points discussed will probably be obvious to them. However, it is in planning that difficulties are experienced and a list of desirable features is considered beneficial for checking plans or reconsidering existing kitchens.

KITCHEN SITE

With regard to site, the following points should be given special emphasis:

(a) The site must be adjacent to the dining room/restaurant.

(b) It must be convenient for delivery from back door to stores to kitchen.

(c) The cost of laying down cables and pipes for electricity and gas must be considered.

(d) It must be above the main sewer to allow gravity flow.

(e) The goods inwards should be accessible from the main road with a loading platform of 3 ft 6 in.

(f) The aspect deserves special consideration both from the dining room/restaurant outlook and from the positioning of the vegetable store, larder and dry stores which should face east or north.

KITCHEN SHELL

The main factors to be considered under this heading are lighting and ventilation, floors and walls and ceilings.

Lighting and ventilation

Both should be natural, the former either from a skylight or high windows.

Floors

Floors must be hard wearing, easy to clean, non-slippery and non-absorbent to grease. Resilience is especially important as they should not be easily damaged or discoloured by hot utensils, cleaning or weight of equipment. With regard to this, thermoplastic tiles or other hard-wearing acrylic tiles may be more suitable than quarry tiles and certainly are more easily maintained and replaced.

Walls and ceilings

These should have a smooth surface, either tiles or glossy paint, and be steam resistant. In addition, they should be lined with materials of low thermal capacity to provide insulation and reduce condensation.

The height of the ceiling should be 12–14 ft for cleaning and fresh-air circulation. Storage ceilings require to be 8–10 ft high.

VENTILATION

General points to be noted are as follows:

  (a) Air must be changed 20–30 times per hour and must be capable of adjustment for peak periods.

  (b) Store rooms and ancillary rooms should not be steam pockets.

  (c) Hoods or extractor fans must be placed over each item of gas-burning equipment.

Natural ventilation

The ventilation should allow the air to be circulated as frequently as described above and air circulation must not depend on draughts.

Hoods

Hoods are required to be high enough to allow comfortable work. They should fit exactly over the equipment area so that staff are not working in a pocket of hot air. These points are illustrated in *Figure 14.1*. In addition, they should have a lip to collect condensation.

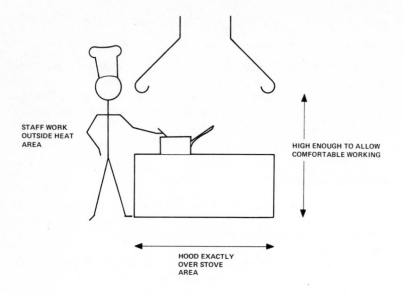

STAFF WORK
OUTSIDE HEAT
AREA

HIGH ENOUGH TO ALLOW
COMFORTABLE WORKING

HOOD EXACTLY
OVER STOVE
AREA

Figure 14.1. Position of hood

Pressure fans

There should be two types of pressure fan: those at low level, forcing air in, and those at high level, taking air out. Extractors must be stronger than input fans and must have washable filters.

LIGHTING

Natural and artificial light must be utilised separately or in combination to minimise shadowing (*Figure 14.2*). For example, this is particularly so with regard to hood shadowing.

In addition, there should be good lighting on boiling tables and fish fryers and the colour of light strips or bulbs must be chosen so as to affect food colours the least. Doors, e.g. oven doors, must open to allow maximum light inside.

HEATING

The following are the main points to be noted with regard to heating:

(a) There should be good insulation of selected equipment.

(b) Air conditioning should be included in the ventilation system.

(c) Heating must be adjusted for special areas such as vegetable preparation, pot-wash, etc.

(d) The kitchen must be at least 50°F when the work begins in the morning.

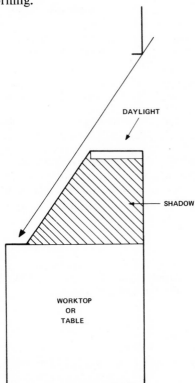

Figure 14.2. Example of shadowing effect

ALLOCATION OF SPACE

The total kitchen area should conform to the scheme shown in *Table 14.1*. Toilets, offices and stores should be $33\frac{1}{3}\%$ of total area.

LAYOUT OF EQUIPMENT

Layout of equipment is an important factor and worth some careful thought. There are several general points to be considered. For example, it must be ensured that materials flow forward to the hot plate and do not criss-cross. Pieces of equipment which are common to many jobs should be situated in the most advantageous position

Table 14.1 Kitchen area allocation

Number of meals	Total area, ft²			
	School meals	Industrial catering	Hotel dining room	Haute cuisine
100	500	600	700	850
250	1 250	1 500	1 750	2 125
500	2 500	3 000	3 500	4 250
750	3 750	4 500	5 350	6 375
1 000	5 000	6 000	7 000	8 500

so that they are accessible from all necessary directions. Equipment must be arranged in the order of preparation and cooking sequences and ancillary rooms placed in the correct work-flow sequence. In addition, further lighting may be necessary at work points.

Wall layout

There must be adequate space allowed for the cleaning of walls, floors and pipes at the back of the equipment.

Centre island

Provision must be made for cleaning between items of equipment.

Storage

The following should be noted:

(a) There should be 5 ft² per diner available in the larder.

(b) There should be 6 in² per diner available in the kitchen dry store.

(c)   There must be sufficient storage for bread and cake, meat and vegetables.

(d)   A store may be more easily accessible from a door opening to the outside, e.g. into a corridor or to the outside of the building, rather than having to transport goods across the kitchen.

EQUIPMENT

General points to be noted with regard to equipment are that:

(a)   The design should facilitate easy cleaning.

(b)   The manufacturer should guarantee adequate maintenance arrangements.

(c)   Shelves should be able to be withdrawn and inserted easily.

Doors

The question of whether a side door is preferable to a drop door is debatable, although drop doors may cause burns. A side door should be able to open more than 90°.

Oven

The manufacturer should guarantee the insulation properties of the oven. The shelves should be sufficiently low or high enough for easy access and enable cooks to reach in easily.

PLANNING TECHNIQUES

One or two visual aids and work study methods used in planning may be helpful in kitchen-planning projects.

Magnetic planning board

These boards are produced from sheet metal permanently magnetised. The board is graduated in measurements scaled to ft². Appliances correctly reduced to scale are superimposed upon the layout so that many alternative arrangements may be considered. The actual size and shape of the kitchen may also be drawn on the board and the optimum layout of equipment arrived at, as illustrated in

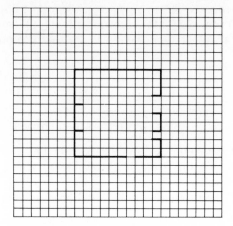

Figure 14.3. Kitchen layout superimposed on planning board

Figure 14.3. The boards and the equipment magnets are obtainable from The Gas Council and are approximately £8 per set.

String diagram

String diagrams (*Figure 14.4*) are a useful adjunct to flow chart procedures and simply show the movement of people between different points.

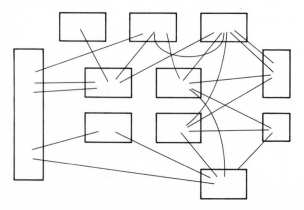

Figure 14.4. String diagram

15
Personnel administration

Personnel administration is a function which exists to satisfy the needs of people at work. As well as personal needs, this embraces union negotiations and consideration of work conditions. Any investigation of successful organisations in and out of catering would show several common factors, one of which would be a dynamic personnel strategy.

For an industry with a greater level of vacancies than most, it is surprising that the personnel function does not assume greater importance. An obvious reason could be the size of the operating units, which tend to be very small and where specific strategy might seem to be unnecessary. The size of the unit, however, is of no consequence; the personnel function must work even if it is (as it frequently must be) carried out by a manager or his assistant in conjunction with other duties.

Staff are selective about the companies for whom they work, and their consideration of a new job will be based largely upon benefits other than money or money's worth, including the opportunity to be rewarded in relation to their effectiveness. Many caterers have the view that their staff work only for money and the quality of personnel relations varies directly with the amount of money they are paid. This is a sad and bigoted view quoted in the main by people who are unsuccessful in building enthusiasm and who are only able to retain staff by paying inflated wages.

The objectives of the personnel function are varied, but their ultimate aim is the maintenance of a happy and enthusiastic staff. Achievement of this is rather difficult but the personnel strategy*

* FEARN, D. A., *Management Systems for the Hotel, Catering and Allied Industries*, Business Books, London (1969)—Labour Strategy.

is the short-term plan of action devised to attain such set objectives. Every owner or manager should consider these principles of personnel strategy as each must apply to their business in some degree.

GUIDE TO THE FORMULATION OF PERSONNEL STRATEGY

Logically, a successful personnel strategy will be based upon the staff requirements in the place of work, and, therefore, these must be specified. The following list is generally thought to be comprehensive:

(a) Security: contract, pensions, other long-term considerations.

(b) Wages, accommodation and feeding.

(c) Opportunities for promotion.

(d) Justice in staff/management relations.

(e) Status of job position.

(f) Knowing what is going on.

(g) Leadership.

(h) Getting the job done.

(i) Interest in and pride of product.

(j) Suggestion schemes.

(k) Joint consultation.

(l) Supplementary benefits.

The food and beverage departments employ the most itinerant staff of the hotel and catering industry. These staff have considerable choice of employment as nearly every establishment in the industry works below its full quota. Therefore, it is important that an operation develops a sound strategy aimed at reducing staff turnover and maintaining a full quota of employees. Such a highly competitive situation demands that, in terms of staff, caterers should provide benefits other than money to retain a contented staff.

Generally, the industry has accepted most management practices easily. However, except for some isolated cases, obtaining and maintaining of staff has been no less than barbaric. There have been many examples of personnel maltreatment by management, in a great number of cases where the companies concerned are household names and management is considered to be good. If an organisation is to have meaningful relationship with its staff any unethical practices must be eliminated.

Security

Most people like to be secure in the knowledge that the company employing them finds them competent in their work and is hopeful of retaining their services for some time. However, all too often this has resulted from the company's fear of perhaps having to pay redundancy money, and a voluntary desire to show employees consideration. More effective methods are necessary in addition.

Some companies have the term 'permanent staff' to denote those employees who satisfactorily complete perhaps six months' employment with them. These have additional benefits, including longer periods of notice, pension rights, and other indications of trust so that the employee knows precisely where he stands with the employer.

Hiring and firing may be convenient, but is very expensive in the long run and a reputation for the habit soon spreads. Any employee who requires security will not be interested in a prospective employer who may dismiss him at a minute's notice, as still happens very frequently. Some managers believe that a high staff turnover and use of hire and fire techniques to be inevitable in the hotel and catering industry. This can be disproved by visiting hotels where a number of staff have been employed for many years. In fact, the *Lygon Arms* at Broadway has so many long-serving members that they have a 'Stalwarts' Club' for all staff of over 10 years' service. The club consists of 25% of the hotel staff. The *Imperial Hotel*, Torquay has some very handsome plaques in the foyer noting the names of staff who have served for twenty, thirty and forty years.

Many other establishments can claim the same success and the fact remains that it can be achieved by management who realise the benefit of providing security for their employees.

Wages, accommodation and feeding

WAGES

Economies in wage costs relate far more to the effectiveness of work done rather than the level of wages paid. Many of the jobs in the industry remain extremely poorly paid whilst others are very highly paid, inflated by gratuities, etc. A company requiring competent employees must expect to pay the market rate in their location. There is no reason, however, to pay 'danger money' to employees who are joining with the expectation that they may be fired at any moment. This assumes that the other components of the personnel strategy are present.

As has been said, many companies are still paying a basic wage which is extremely low and supplement it with the proportion of the service charge applicable to the employee in a particular week. It is unfair to expect someone to work not knowing what their wage is to be until they open the envelope. Certainly, wages tend to be high in the summer and low in the winter, and over a year an average weekly wage would be a reasonable sum. However, the fluctuation caused does create problems in an individual's budget and commitments, especially if he has very heavy credit arrangements such as mortgages and car repayments.

The most equitable method of payment is to guarantee a weekly wage based upon the total annual wage and service charge amount.

STAFF FEEDING

Staff feeding may be considered from a number of viewpoints:

(a) It may be a method of getting rid of all the waste items which the kitchen cannot use for any other purpose.

(b) Reducing the cost of staff feeding is one way of effectively dealing with complaints regarding the food cost of sales percentages. This can be done by serving very cheap food continuously.

(c) The cost of staff feeding may be played off against the allowance to absorb high prices and other irregularities.

It must never be forgotten that most staff rely on staff feeding (especially in hotels) for their main food intake, and for that reason care should be taken to ensure that meals are balanced and nutritious as well as maintaining interest. The only way to achieve this is to have a staff-feeding menu based on a ten-day cycle. In addition, items left over from banquets or the restaurant may be served but these must never be the main component of staff feeding. It has been known for operations to serve such items as egg and chips for staff lunch for long periods of time. One particular establishment did this for six weeks. Not surprisingly, staff turnover rose rapidly during that period.

STAFF ACCOMMODATION

Staff accommodation is much like staff food, in that luxury is not expected, but clean, reasonably sized, warm rooms should not be too much to ask. One very well-known hotel manager takes the view that the first item of maintenance expenditure should be the staff rooms, because he believes that a happy staff make up for many shortcomings in decorations. Again, it should be remembered that the room is 'home' for most hotel staff and if it is thoroughly unattractive, unhealthy or too small it is not reasonable to expect them to move house . . . and job.

Opportunities for promotion

The size of units in the UK catering industry (80% are single, independent units) precludes many levels of staff from promotion because the jobs are just not available. This means that unit operators

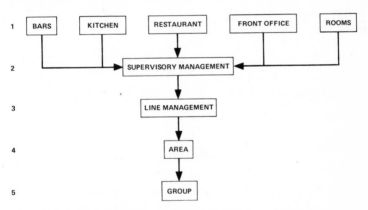

Figure 15.1. Promotion prospects in catering organisations

must accept that their staff will leave for better jobs after one or two years, except in rare cases where they are content to keep the same job without any enlargment of responsibility. Generally, the latter applies to married women, although in some cases it might not.

The main problem in creating promotion opportunities is the number of diverse departments in even the smallest establishment. *Figure 15.1* shows this, the promotion gap being between 1 and 2— 2–5 being an acceptable progression. The difficulty arises when a member of staff has become head of a department through exercising a good craft knowledge and an industrial or natural flair for fore-manship. The gap between this and supervisory management (food and beverage or rooms) is a large one and may only be solved by expensive experience (a risk that most caterers are unwilling to take) or a relevant training programme (which does not currently exist for this purpose).

It is hoped that training programmes, preferably 'sandwich' courses, could be evolved by the HCITB to bridge this gap. They would tend to be based on the structure shown in *Figure 15.2.* Should the possibility of progression on a merit basis from a hotel department to group management become established, then hotel keeping and catering as a career would become more attractive to young men and women.

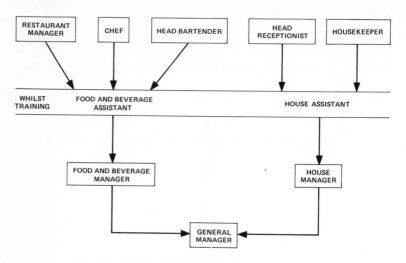

Figure 15.2. Training programme structure

As a matter of interest there is one general manager of a large quoted hotel group who started as a kitchen porter, and a professor at Cornell University who commenced his catering career as a bell-hop.

Justice in staff/management relations

It is probably true to say that most people do not mind accepting the consequences of their own mistakes. However, they would feel a sense of gross injustice if they were expected to accept responsibility for mistakes which were not theirs, however trivial.

It is extremely important that management should be just at all times. Even the 'dictator-type' managers, of whom the industry has not a few, retain respect and loyalty from their staff if they are just. In fact, employees will nearly always describe a new manager firstly by virtue of his fairness or otherwise.

That justice works in both directions is evidenced by the equally righteous expostulations of management and unions in industries where labour is 'organised'. Obviously what is considered just for one is not necessarily just for another. For example, a company which is being wound up cannot be expected to pay large sums of compensation to employees; however, it is considered unfair on employees to change their jobs and possibly trade, at short notice. In this instance, the State enters the situation as a third party to dispense unemployment pay collected from both employee and employer alike over a period of years.

Some common corporate problems may be settled by the State. However, the attitudes of management in their dealings with staff are internal to the business and little aid is obtained from outside. Some companies do enable members of staff to appeal to a higher authority—this, of course, intimates a breakdown in management relationships and must lead to an impossible situation, especially if the appeal goes against the subordinate manager.

The only adequate way to deal with the situation is to ensure that line management are fully aware of the importance of administering in a just manner. Nothing will reduce morale and enthusiasm faster than evidence of unfairness with its consequent extremely serious effect on work and indeed profitability. For example, in one operation, a grievance held by the restaurant management against head office caused profits to dip drastically in one week after four months of good results. The management of food and beverage profits is a delicate operation requiring the full and continuous attention of line management; should this attention wander or become focused upon some grievance or other the effect will become apparent in the figures before very long.

No manager should set out to be unfair. Evidence of unfairness usually occurs because:

(a) Management is dealing with too many other 'important' things to be concerned about staff problems.

(b) Because of lack of time, management does not consider a decision properly and takes incorrect action.

(c) Because of panic or confusion, a snap decision is made just to *remove* the problem rather than eliminate it.

The basic rule is that until the facts have been investigated and clarified, the manager should refrain from reaching any decision.

Status of job position

A man can spend over 40% of his time in his place of work, especially if he works over 45 hours per week. It is, therefore, natural that he should feel that the work he does is deserving of some status in the organisation. This applies in a proportionately greater degree as employees move up the line, passing through one status by dint of skill or hard work to another.

Most far-sighted managers give subordinates their due in written and verbal communication as well as in meetings of management and staff. It must be remembered that a successful operation must be run by a team, which will not provide a co-ordinated effort if status and responsibility commensurate with the job are not given.

Status is the public award of responsibility (as seen by the work team). It may be given without responsibility, as in the case of many hotel assistant managers, but this tends to be a most unsatisfactory situation because the holder of the position becomes frustrated and either sits back or gives notice. Responsibility without status is as bad. Staff feel that due recognition is not given to their work and usefulness to the business, and, consequently, do not take their responsibilities as seriously as they might.

Status is important to a man in his place of work and thus management should see that both status and responsibility are awarded to personnel. One cannot readily understand the feelings of certain managements who insist on a mixture of both for no apparent purpose.

Knowing what is going on

Contrary to the ideas of most managements, subordinates do like to know what is happening in terms of management. This knowledge stimulates a greater commitment from the personnel and a more ready identification with the business.

In addition to the frank and open discussions of plans and performance, the use of incentive bonuses based on performance is incorporated by many organisations to encourage commitment and enthusiasm more readily. Some of the most effective are based on a proportion of net profit over budget, or food costs, liquor costs and wages costs.

MANAGEMENT BONUS

Table 15.1 shows a restaurant trading account for June, 1972. The management bonus is calculated on 10% of the surplus between

Table 15.1 Restaurant trading account

Sales	Actual, £	%	Budget, £	%
Food	20 000	67	17 000	67
Liquor	10 000	33	8 500	33
Total	30 000	100	25 500	100
Food cost	6 200	31	5 100	30
Liquor cost	4 000	40	3 570	42
Total cost	10 200	34	8 670	34
Gross margin	19 800	66	16 830	·66
Wages	4 500	15	4 800	18
Net margin	15 300	51	12 030	48
Overhead	1 000	3	1 100	4
Net profit	14 300	48	10 930	44

the actual profit and budgeted profit. In this case, it is £337. The proportion received by each of the managers and assistants is shown in *Table 15.2*.

Table 15.2 Managers' and assistants' bonuses

Staff	£p
Managers	
Mr. A at	112·34
Mr. B at	112·34
Assistants	
Mr. C at	56·17
Mr. D at	56·17

FOOD BONUS

The bonus on food cost is computed as shown in *Table 15.3*. As the food cost percentage in the example is 31 %, then the chef would earn a bonus of £16 for the month.

Table 15.3 Food bonus calculation

Food cost, %	Food cost, %
28	12
29	16
30	20
31	16
32	12

LIQUOR BONUS

Liquor bonuses are normally computed on the basis of surpluses earned in the same way as food. However, sales mix will alter the rate of surplus earned normally by between $2\frac{1}{2}\%$ and 5%, and occasionally higher. *Table 15.4* shows the calculation of bonuses for cocktail bars. The bonus will be paid to the staff operating each bar.

It must be remembered that the amount of bonus paid on food and liquor above depends largely on the turnover of the operation and

Table 15.4 Bar bonus calculation

Cocktail bar	Surplus, % dispense	Bonus, £
3	$1\frac{1}{2}$	12
4	2	16
5	$2\frac{1}{2}$	20
6	3	16
7	$3\frac{1}{2}$	12

that bonuses reduce over a certain level in order to discourage staff from short-portioning.

PAYROLL BONUS

Where management are not responsible for net profit, a payroll bonus is occasionally used, based either on total savings or budget. The amount paid is normally 10% of savings.

Leadership

The ability to lead is often considered a natural gift. But analysis of the skills involved indicate that it may be acquired. Also, it has certain basic components which are as follows:

(*a*) Never do anything one would not want one's staff to do.

(*b*) Recognise that familiarity breeds contempt.

(*c*) Maintain an interest in the affairs of subordinates, e.g. with regard to weddings, illnesses, etc.

(*d*) Be approachable for private consultations.

This would seem to be a very simple personal managerial policy to conform to, but many people in management never achieve the right balance. Basically, it is a simple matter of recognising the rules and adhering to them. Leadership is neither achieved by a father-figure nor a tyrant.

Getting the job done

Whatever duties are held by catering staff it is important that management instils a need to have the job done in the correct manner. This is, in fact, an extension of leadership in that management should encourage staff to have a pride in their own work and the efficiency with which they carry out that work.

Obviously, one can carry this out through induction and on-the-job training, but what is more important is the continuous wish by the individual to improve his or her skill. Contrary to some management's thinking, staff do react beneficially to encouragement in the right way—and the right way is to provide a challenge. The majority of people like to be thought of as good at their job and need only a little encouragement to show that they are. On the other hand, management which does not appear interested will stimulate carelessness and disinterest on the part of their staff. There are, of course, those who cannot achieve any interest in the job they do and this, inevitably, shows up in their performance. Staff in this category usually cause more trouble for other people than make a job contribution, and they may be better off elsewhere or doing another job.

Some companies award prizes through competitions for the best receptionist, waiter, housekeeper and so on. For the small operator this would be ludicrous, but he does have the advantage of personally supervising his staff.

Interest in and pride of product

Both management and employees will be happier if all personnel are interested in the establishment for which they work and are proud of what they accomplish. One does not need to own a large hotel to expect this, but every establishment has an individual character whatever it may be.

A prerequisite to the stimulation of pride in the product is knowledge of what is going on in terms of changes, new plans, promotions, and, of course, operating performance. Apart from achieving free promotion through an extra number of salesmen (the attitude will be reflected in customer relations), staff will feel more secure and, therefore, more interested in their work.

An examination of companies with very good performance will, inevitably, include a majority with sound personnel strategies. It is obvious that any company with one or two men at the top providing the total dynamism of the organisation cannot be as effective as a company where *all* the staff are contributing to it.

Suggestion schemes

Some managements consider it tantamount to insult for staff to suggest improvements that they have not thought of first. However, it is logical to assume that if staff specialise in a particular, repetitive function in a particular part of the building then they have a far better opportunity than management of knowing every disadvantage of the job and methods of improving it. By encouraging suggestions from staff on improvements, management obtains a ready flow of cost reduction ideas. Many companies give a reward for good suggestions, which, of course, encourages the flow rather more.

Nothing is more discouraging to staff than a suggestion scheme which is abortive. Therefore, before starting it is essential to realise that, once initiated, it will become an established procedure.

Joint consultation

As much as personnel require to be kept informed about future plans and performance, it is as important to consult them on certain other matters, e.g. pay, hours of work, conditions, etc. In practice, it is useful to have a regular meeting and to use the meeting as a sounding board for future plans and changes, as well as personnel matters.

The composition of the meeting will depend upon the establishment. Normally, a group will hold a meeting of managers and possibly assistants; subsequent meetings will be held by unit managers with representatives of each department. The information arising at each meeting will be passed back up the line for consideration.

Supplementary benefits

Many organisations give extra benefits to personnel, such as non-contributory pension schemes, motor cars, shopping discount clubs, share participation schemes, staff clubs, help on mortgage interest rates, etc. Some benefits are more easily provided than others, and, indeed, some companies provide none at all. But most substantial catering companies at least have, or are seriously considering having, pension schemes.

If the company is large enough to afford perquisites such as those described above then they certainly have an advantage in obtaining and keeping personnel. However, these items are frequently looked upon as salary, and, therefore, very careful consideration must be given before adjusting or discontinuing them.

PERSONNEL AND TRAINING

As can be seen from the above, the personnel and training functions are extremely close, if not combined activities. In fact, greater benefit to the company will be obtained by closely co-ordinating both, so that training is geared to the right people at the right time.

CONCLUSION

It would appear that the hotel and catering industry contains a large number of itinerant workers. There are exceptions, however, and some establishments achieve a very low staff turnover. Therefore, it must be concluded that staff try a number of establishments before settling down, and it is those establishments with a dynamic personnel strategy which retain them.

16
Control

The function of control in hotels and catering establishments is to ensure that goods purchased are converted into cash and that cash taken makes its way safely into the bank account. To illustrate the control function, *Figure 16.1* shows the movement of cash through the departments of an operation and isolates each control area which may allow cash outflows (fraud).

CASH AT BANK

The greater the credit balance of cash at bank, the greater is the amount available for additional investment, or for assisting in bad times. Should the company operate an overdraft on which it pays high interest rates, conservation of cash becomes doubly important.

Turn-round of cash

Cash is more useful to the caterer if it is turned round faster. If large sums are moving slowly (debtors/stock) they may make a considerable difference to the amount of cash at bank available to operate the business. The documents required to control the use of cash are the forecast cash flow and balance sheet, both of which have been discussed in Chapter 13.

PURCHASE OF BUILDINGS AND EQUIPMENT

Considerable sums of money are wasted by caterers and companies in the purchase or erection of buildings and in the purchase of equipment. It is not pertinent here to discuss detailed consideration of building and equipment costs, but a few points to note are as follows:

(*a*) A feasibility study of the new or existing operation may save considerable sums of cash later. The study should

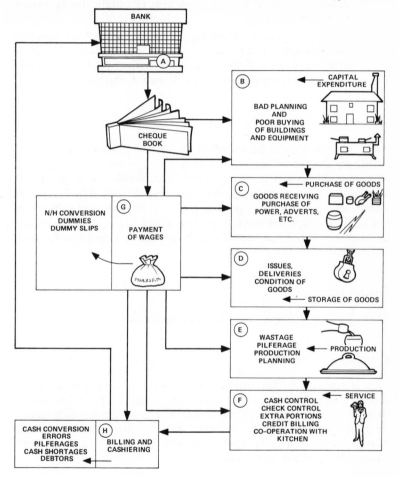

Figure 16.1. The 'money-go-round'

include a detailed assessment of the market, capital costs and financial appraisal.

(*b*) Building costs differ considerably in the UK. Normally, they vary from £10 per ft² depending on materials and design. Also, the choice of one's architect should be made with careful consideration.

(c) Equipment qualities and costs differ enormously; but it is essential to ensure that it has a precise specification and warranty. Many forms of discount may be negotiated for different reasons, so it is important to obtain the maximum wherever possible.

(d) There are several planning techniques useful to hoteliers and caterers in the provision of new operations or alterations to existing ones. Two of these are critical path analysis and PERT (production evaluation review technique).

PURCHASE OF GOODS

All purchases should be specified on official printed order forms, and these should be signed by the buyer. The specified goods will be compared against incoming goods and action taken should the items differ. This procedure is discussed in more detail in Chapter 6. There are, however, a large number of expensive items which do not come through the back door and which are seldom controlled by management. These items are shown below together with their control factor.

Control principles

There are two principles of control applicable to catering.

1. OPERATING CONTROL

This is relevant to the physical movement of cash and materials and is governed by responsibility. For example, every restaurant check has the signature of the waiter who received the dish signed on it. Responsibility may be routed back to particular individuals. This principle normally applies to physical goods such as food, liquor, china, plate, glass, etc.

2. CONTROL FACTOR

Some items, however, are not easily considered in total. For this reason, a control factor is employed. This is a governing ratio applied to the total consumption of such items. For example:

Cost of cleaning

Control factor = square footage
Total cleaning cost   £600
Total square footage, 2 000 ft²
Cost per ft²   60p
Budgeted cost per ft²   50p
       Variance   10p
Budgeted total   £500

Table 16.1 shows the control factors for a number of items.

Table 16.1 Examples of control factors

Item of cost	Control factor
Cleaning supplies	Square footage
Window cleaning	Square foot of glass
Guests' supplies (catering)	Cost per diner
Laundry (catering)	Cost per diner
Linen (catering)	Cost per diner
Telephone charges	Cost per diner
Uniforms	Cost per employee
Staff transport	Cost per employee
Staff advertisements	Cost per employee
Furnishing and equipment hire	Cost per diner
Paper supplies	Cost per diner
Glass	Cost per diner
Books and stationery	Cost per day
Soft furnishings	Cost per diner
Floor coverings	Cost per diner
Menus	Cost per diner
Wine lists	Cost per diner
China	Cost per diner
Kitchen utensils	Cost per diner
Plate	Cost per diner
Staff drink	Cost per employee
Kitchen fuel	Cost per diner
Electricity	Cost per square foot
Gas	Cost per square foot
Oil	Cost per square foot
Other fuel	Cost per square foot
Water	Cost per diner
Flowers	Cost per diner
Band and orchestra	Cost per meal session
Rent payable	Cost per square foot
Rates	Cost per square foot
Insurance	Cost per square foot

STORAGE

The storage of materials is dealt with in detail in Chapter 8 and inclusion of storage in this chapter is relevant only to the conservation of cash. The stores purchased and held should be the minimum amount necessary to allow the business to operate. An effective method of reducing stockholdings is by using 'par stock control' which is discussed further in Chapter 18.

PRODUCTION

Production control often tends to be forgotten by catering management. Goods are carefully controlled from entry to bar or kitchen, and controlled from bar or kitchen to customer, but little control is exercised within production areas. This promotes wastage, pilferage, bad menu planning and over-production.

WAGES

Control of wages is also often ignored until a fraud occurs. The function of wage control is to ensure that all monies drawn from the bank account are used for the payment of sums due to employees and government agencies. The following points should be considered:

(a) Cheques drawn should equal amounts on payroll records. Payroll records should *never* be kept in pencil or by other means which may be easily erased.

(b) Cash should *never* be drawn for NHI stamps. An arrangement should be made with the GPO to obtain stamps in exchange for a crossed cheque drawn to the order of the Postmaster-General.

(c) Wage slips should be a duplicate (carbon or NCR paper copy) of the payroll, and should on no occasion be copied on to other documents. *On no account* should the type of pay packets with wages and deductions written on the outside be used, as tax deductions, etc., may be increased and the cash taken.

(d) Payment of cheques to the Inland Revenue should be undertaken by a person other than the wages clerk.

(e) Wages sheets should be checked for fictitional employees.

BILLING AND CASHIERING

Cash handling should be controlled by a disciplined system, as shown in *Figure 16.2*. From the diagram the following points may be noted:

(*a*) Restaurant and lounge and floor service checks should be changed to customers' bills and sales summary.

(*b*) The customer pays cash to discharge his debt.

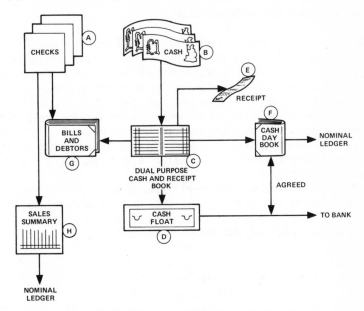

Figure 16.2. Billing and cashiering control system

(*c*) The cash received should be recorded in the *cash/receipt book*. The advantage of this type of cash record is that no sum may be receipted without appearing as a cash record.

(*d*) *The cash till* should be reconciled with *cash/receipt book* and should equal the amount shown therein.

(*e*) The customer receives the *receipt*.

(*f*) The daily total from the *cash/receipt book* should be recorded in the *cash day book*. The monthly total from the *cash/receipt book* should be posted to accounts receivable (debtors) in the nominal ledger.

(*g*) Unpaid bills should be collated as debtors until paid.

(*h*)   The totals from the *sales summary* should be posted to sales accounts and accounts receivable (debtors) in the nominal ledger.

The system is simple and easy to operate. It is, however, so constructed that any normal fraud may be prevented or isolated within a short period.

Large, medium and small operations

Obviously, the degree of sophistication will depend upon the size of the operation. During the autumn of 1969 a study of computer systems for hotel and catering operations was started. The results of these studies indicated that, in the near future, hotels will be able to be 'on line' to a large computer for one or two hours per day through an ordinary teleprinter which will provide inexpensive computing services to many medium and small hotels. ('On line' means to be connected to a computer and passing data to and receiving data from the computer through a connection—in this case a teleprinter.)

The above indicates the sophistication available in terms of control procedures. However, it must be made clear that the method of preparation is of little consequence compared to the type of information produced and the use to which it is put.

MEASURING THE VALUE OF CONTROL INFORMATION

Control information should be measured from the action end; that is its usefulness in increasing efficiency by indicating untoward trends from which a decision may be made and action taken. Therefore, the documents which are considered hereunder should be examined from this point of view.

Checks—the basis of all control procedures

Check systems have been universally the basis of control procedures in catering operations except, of course, for cash-only operations. It is, therefore, important that the purposes of check systems are understood and that procedures based on checks are properly operated. The functions of checks are to provide:

(*a*) A record of the order.

(*b*) A requisition of the goods.

(*c*) Advice to cashier or billing office of charge.

(*d*) A control copy to reconcile total charges to customers.

Some check systems use three copies, others use two. Either system is acceptable provided that copies are not substituted for

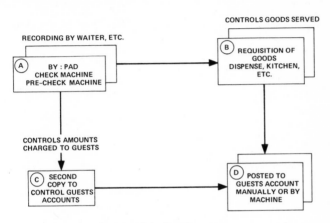

Figure 16.3. Checks system

others in order to obtain cash or goods. These points are summarised in *Figure 16.3*. In addition, the following should also be noted with regard to checks:

(*a*) They should be consecutively numbered.

(*b*) They should be legibly written.

(*c*) They should have cash columns.

(*d*) They should be signed.

(*e*) They should have different colours for different departments.

(*f*) They should be perforated for meal service.

An example of a check is shown in *Figure 16.4*.

Control information for caterers

Table 16.2 summarises the control information required by caterers and the points outlined in the table are discussed below.

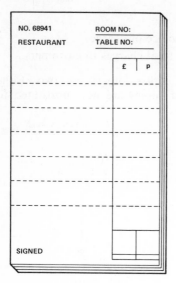

| NO. 68941 | ROOM NO: |
| RESTAURANT | TABLE NO: |

| | £ | p |

SIGNED

Figure 16.4. Example of a check

Table 16.2 Control information for caterers

Control report	*Brief description*
Management accounts	Overall performance, normally produced monthly
Daily sales report	Includes sleepers, covers served, etc.
Wages report	Includes NHI, SET, staff feeding and staff accommodation
Staff turnover report	Rates of departmental turnover
New skills report	Describes new skills achieved by personnel through training
Cash under/over	Record of float shortages and 'overages'
Bad debts and accounts receivable report	Report of credit sales and accounts which have not been collected
Weekly food control report	Varying systems indicating reasons for shortfalls from budgeted gross margin
Liquor stock report	As above
Heat, light, power report	Indicates consumption of gas, electricity, water and oil
Repairs and maintenance	Estimates of maintenance to be undertaken and maintenance carried out

MANAGEMENT ACCOUNTS

Management accounts illustrate the performance of a hotel or catering unit in detail, showing the actual performance compared against budgets.

DAILY SALES REPORT

The daily sales report shows the detailed breakdown of sales with statistical information indicating the effectiveness of the operation. An example of a daily sales report is shown in *Figure 16.5*.

DAILY SALES REPORT	Montcalm Room		16/5/69
Item	£	Av. per diner, £p	
		Today	Budget
Table d'hote	248	1·00	1·00
A la carte	146	2·34	3·00
Wine rack	150	0·47	0·40
Liqueur trolley	50	0·16	0·25
Cocktail bar	75	0·20½	0·35
Total	669	4·17½	5·00
Diners		160	200
Diners: weekly	Total	1 908	2 140
Seat occupancy		76%	87%
Comments:			
		Food and beverage manager	

Figure 16.5. Daily sales report

WAGES REPORT AND STAFF TURNOVER REPORT

The wages report (*Figure 16.6*) is analysed by department and categories of wages burden, to show the true wages burden of each department. The report also includes the turnover of staff in each so that any untoward trends may be isolated.

Nonesuch Hotel　　　　WAGES REPORT　　　　W/E 14/4/69

Department	No.	Gross pay, £	Staff food, £	Staff accomm., £	NHI, SET, £	Total, £	Budget, £	Variance, £	Leavers this week	To date
Kitchen	7	140	14	9	28	191	180	−11	1	3
Stillroom	2	25	4	–	8	37	36	−1	–	2
Plateroom	2	24	4	3	8	39	39	–	2	16
Receiving	1	15	4	–	4	23	23	–	–	–
Reception	2	22	4	3	8	37	35	−2	–	1
Restaurant Waiters	11	165	22	30	44	261	250	−11	3	24
Grill room Waiters	4	60	8	9	16	93	90	−3	2	10
Cocktail bar Barmen	2	38	4	3	8	53	50	−3	1	1
Saloon bar Barmen	2	36	4	–	8	48	48	–	–	1
Total	33	£525	£68	£57	£132	£782	£751	−£31	9	58

Figure 16.6. Wages report

NEW SKILLS REPORT

The recent emphasis on training in the hotel and catering industry, which has been brought about by the compulsory payment of a training levy, has resulted in the formal training of many categories of staff. Hitherto, their training has been simply a case of 'watching other people'.

Although many people become trained in new skills within large organisations, management is seldom aware of this and, consequently, many members of staff and management are unable to use their newly acquired skills. By circulating reports periodically showing what skills have been acquired by whom, management is able to consider transfers and promotions in the light of this, thus making their training programme work for them.

The report will not be produced in any specific format but will include the following information:

(a) Name of employee.

(b) Age.

(c) Course of training.

(d) Length of time current position held.

(e) Length of time with company.

(f) Where presently employed.

(g) Position.

(h) Assessment of training result.

(i) Immediate superior.

CASH SHORTAGES/'OVERAGES' REPORT

This report will be simple in design and may be incorporated in the design of other reports, e.g. the cash takings sheet or the cash day book, etc. It is important that cash floats are made the direct responsibility of the person using them so that shortages or overages may be identified in terms of the cashier using the float.

An example of this report incorporated into the cash day book is shown in *Figure 16.7*.

ACCOUNTS RECEIVABLE AND BAD DEBTS REPORT

The credit squeezes of the past few years have obliged businessmen to give careful consideration to the number of debtors outstanding.

A monthly report of accounts receivable and bad debts is essential to every hotelier and caterer so that debts may be kept at a reasonable level.

Many companies operate a debtors' cycle and allow a certain period for this. The advantage of controlling debtors in this way

CASH DAY BOOK			Month	
Date	Receipt book, £p	Bank book, £p	Variance, £p	Banked by
1	520·52½	520·52½	–	J Brown
2	480·28	481·12	+0·82	D Evans
3	328·00	328·00	–	J Brown
4	296·52	297·52	+1·00	J Brown
5	313·00	313·00	–	D Evans
6	408·00	407·13	−0·82	J Brown
7				
8				
9				
10				
11				
12				
⋮				
29				
30				
31				
Total				

Figure 16.7. Cash day book and shortages/overages report

is that the cycle may be used for forecast cash flow purposes. A typical debtors' cycle is shown in *Figure 16.8*.

Bill sent (1)	State- ment (2)	Chaser 1 (3)	Chaser 2 (4)	Chaser 3 (5)	Final letter (6)	
Day after the account	10th day of fol- lowing month	End of follow- ing month	Two weeks after (3)	Two weeks after (4)	Two weeks after (5)	BAD DEBT
	10 days	41 days	55 days	69 days	83 days	

Figure 16.8. Debtors' cycle

The accounts receivable report (*Figure 16.9*) is tabulated to conform to the debtors' cycle so that management are able to assess the speed at which debts are likely to be settled.

Heat, light, power

Hotel and catering establishments use large quantities of power (varying between 3 and 5% of turnover) for many different purposes and in differing departments. Because of the ease with which power

BAD DEBTS/ACCOUNTS RECEIVABLE as at								30/6/69	
Name	Statement	1	2	3	4	5	6	Bad debts	Total
Total									

Figure 16.9. Accounts receivable report

charges may rise when, e.g., close-down routines are ignored, lights are left on, or boiler pumps do not cut out, it is important that management are aware of the heat, light and power consumption month by month. This may be done in the form of a heat, light and power consumption report, as shown in *Figure 16.10*.

The charges made by power suppliers may be controlled by comparison with this report. Target amounts may be obtained from heating and ventilating engineers and electrical engineers for comparison purposes.

REPAIRS AND MAINTENANCE

Repairs and maintenance accounts for a large proportion of the turnover of a hotel or catering establishment if it is being fully maintained. By full maintenance is meant:

(a) Repairs necessary to maintain a fully effective operation.

(b) Expenditure on all operations to ensure modernity and progress with the times.

Department	Gas, ft³	Oil, gal	Water, '000 gal	Electricity, units	Total
Kitchen fuel	X				X
Gas fires, staff house	X				X
Central heating and hot water		X	X		X
Electricity				X	X
Electricity, staff house				X	X
Total	X	X	X	X	X

Figure 16.10. Heat, light and power consumption report

Maintenance reports will show the estimated expenditure for a future year, and items will be updated monthly to indicate whether expenditure is likely to exceed estimates. The report will normally include expenditure on renewals on the same basis. Normally repairs and maintenance accounts for 5 to 7% of turnover and renewals from 1 to 3% of turnover.

There is no ideal system of control information for any hotel or catering establishment as it depends upon a number of factors. These are:

(a) The ability of management to interpret and take action upon the information produced.

(b) The products and departments operated.

(c) The size of the establishment.

(d) The cost of operating the system relative to the savings obtainable.

   Consideration of the above factors will allow management to determine the nature and requirements of the operation and thus enable them to make decisions regarding the type and volume of control information necessary. There is little truth in the oft-repeated phrase 'over-control is as bad as no control'. However, staff may easily become overloaded where profitability does not justify, for example, further clerical staff. They will also become apathetic towards the compilation of information which is not used for any worthwhile purpose and will become careless in correcting errors or leave out important sections of the work which will render the information useless. Most operations, however, employ far too little control with a resulting considerable annual loss of cash.

17
Food control

Obviously, food cost control is extremely important to the hotel and catering industry, but, unfortunately, there is space to describe only one or two methods of control. However, the principles of food transactions are shown so that variations of the systems illustrated may be applied.

The main function of all control systems is to ensure that each transaction (operation) is adequately documented. This is best considered if it is remembered that control points are only necessary where movement of goods takes place or where the goods are used for some purpose. *Figure 17.1* shows the various transactions which occur and the variances which may result at each point.

Many of the areas shown on the diagram have been discussed in previous chapters, e.g., receival, storage, etc. They will be referred to below only in so far as they are relevant to food control systems.

THE MENU

Most control systems seem to ignore the menu assuming that, as far as control is concerned, it is correct. A badly planned menu, i.e. a menu in which the mix of dishes offered is totally unrelated to the market, will erode gross profit immediately.

EXAMPLE

Figure 17.2 shows a typical table d'hôte menu. If, on any one day, menu items sold were as shown in *Table 17.1* and on a subsequent day as shown in *Table 17.2*, it will be seen that the same menu at the same component prices returns a gross profit which is as much as 9% different. In a small hotel selling £20 000 of food per annum,

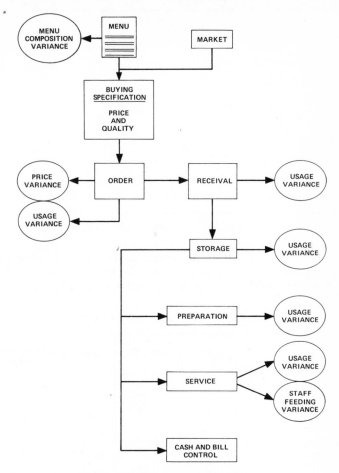

Figure 17.1. Food transactions diagram

such a percentage loss of gross profit would equal a loss in profit of £1 800—a not inconsiderable sum.

Any adequate food control system must, therefore, indicate gross profit loss caused by bad menu planning separately from other loss areas. In the system of food control advocated here, this is known as the menu composition variance. Food and beverage managers must pay particular attention to the composition variance as the success of future menu mixes depends on it. Frequently, the menu composition variance shows a large credit amount, which

---

Luncheon, £

Starters	Cost of dish, p
Dish 1	14
Dish 2	3
Dish 3	20

Main course	
Dish 1	$52\frac{1}{2}$
Dish 2	$17\frac{1}{2}$
Dish 3	25

Sweets	
Dish 1	$4\frac{1}{2}$
Dish 2	$7\frac{1}{2}$
Dish 3	$1\frac{1}{2}$

Figure 17.2. Typical table d'hôte menu

artificially inflates gross profit considerably. A hotel producing a gross profit of 69%, may well be obtaining 6% of it from a favourable menu composition variance and perhaps be losing elsewhere.

Table 17.1 Menu items sold on Day 1

Dish	Sales	Cost, £p	Selling, £	Gross profit, £p
Starter				
Dish 1	10	$1\cdot37\frac{1}{2}$		
Dish 2	4	$11\frac{1}{2}$		
Dish 3	3	60		
Main course				
Dish 1	4	$2\cdot10$		
Dish 2	3	$52\frac{1}{2}$		
Dish 3	10	$2\cdot50$		
Sweet				
Dish 1	8	34		
Dish 2	—	—		
Dish 3	2	$2\frac{1}{2}$		
Total		£7·58	17·00	$8\cdot42\frac{1}{2}$ (55%)

This is a situation in which a poor menu which does not give value for money is supporting other loss areas such as pilferage, wastage, etc.

BUYING SPECIFICATIONS

When the market has been assessed, the menu designed and the quality and price decided, buying specifications may then be produced. This may be done in a number of ways, e.g. by using notices, manuals,

Table 17.2 Menu items sold on Day 2

Dish	Sales	Cost, £p	Selling, £	Gross profit, £p
Starter				
Dish 1	4	55		
Dish 2	10	29		
Dish 3	3	60		
Main course				
Dish 1	12	6·25		
Dish 2	5	87		
Dish 3	—	—		
Sweet				
Dish 1	2	8		
Dish 2	6	45		
Dish 3	2	2½		
Total		£9·11½	17·00	7·87

kitchen blackboards. These methods of presentation seldom work in catering because pressure of work frequently obliges staff to dispense with them. A much more reliable alternative is the standard order form, the object of which is to continually bring prices and other factors of specification before staff at the time of order. The standard order form has already been described in Chapter 6 and an example is shown in *Figure 6.2*, page 67.

Factors to be included in the buying specification are:

(*a*) *Meat.* Price per lb, cut, quality.

(*b*) *Poultry.* Price per lb, clean weight or not, quality, size of bird.

(*c*) *Dry goods.* Price per pack, size of pack, quality, weight.

ORDERING AND DELIVERIES

When items have been ordered according to the buying specification, it is important that the goods ordered are, in fact, delivered. Many caterers take adequate precautions to ensure that orders are placed accurately, but do not make certain that those goods are actually delivered. The system advocated is that standard order forms are passed to the receiving office so that incoming goods may be checked off against them. Receiving procedures and requisitions have already been discussed in Chapters 6 and 7.

PREPARATION

The dishes that management advertise on the menu must be those prepared by the kitchen. In order to do this a 'dish specification card' is produced for each dish on the menu. This lays down the weight of each item used for making up 1, 5, 50, and 100 portions of specific dishes, the standard price of each item and, therefore, the standard cost per dish.

SERVICE

The service of food frequently invites loss of goods and revenue if checking systems are inadequate. Care should be taken to ensure that every item served by the kitchen is backed by a check which can be traced to cash or a charge to a bill.

STANDARD FOOD COST CONTROL

Having discussed the principles of food control, the system is shown in detail in *Figure 17.3*, so that the documentation involved may be considered.

Ordering goods

Food should be ordered so that it is delivered within the succeeding few days. In some cases the chef may order, but this should only be done under the supervision of management. The order may be made by telephone, in writing, or by a daily order, e.g. milk, cream or bread rolls.

Whichever method of ordering is used, every item must be written up on the standard order form. Prices may be negotiated either at the time of ordering or by weekly suppliers' lists, or they may not be known until invoiced.

CALCULATING STANDARD PRICES

Use of the standard order form necessitates that the manager first checks on the current prices of goods to be ordered. The following

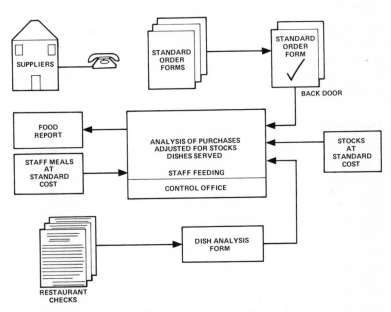

Figure 17.3. Standard food cost control

information will then be recorded on the standard order form: (*a*) the agreed price for the goods; (*b*) the amount ordered (number or weight).

Standard prices of commodities are based upon market trends and interviews with suppliers regarding likely trends over the forthcoming twelve months. An average price for the year is assessed and allocated to the goods on the standard order form. This is, obviously, a skilled job and those people that undertake it should be knowledgeable of market price trends and quality.

Receiving office (back door)

The standard order forms are passed to the receiving office where they are filed under the names of suppliers. When the goods arrive they are checked against delivery note/invoice by the receiving clerk. Normally, suppliers are encouraged to send priced delivery notes or invoices with their deliveries so that actual prices may be checked against negotiated prices by the clerk. The goods are also checked against the standard order form to ensure that the amount and quality supplied are similar to those ordered.

Analysis of purchases

The standard order forms are passed to the control office who extend purchases at actual and standard prices and calculate the price variance, if any. The price variances are summarised as shown in *Figure 17.4*. Large operations summarise daily whilst smaller operations summarise weekly.

Stocktaking

The standard order forms are used for stocktaking, as they constitute a checklist of all items purchased by the organisation. As the standard prices are noted on the form the stock at standard cost may be easily calculated. Stocks are normally taken weekly to provide a weekly food report. There is no reason why food reports should be produced less frequently, other than the fact that variances become more difficult to isolate over periods longer than a week. Further, the volume of food turnover in comparison with potential losses demands that variances should be isolated within a very short period.

A variation of the system can be employed if a large dry store is kept. A separate stores ledger (*Figure 17.5*) will be opened for each item and kept up to date by recording requisitions and deliveries. The stock balance will be controlled by physical stocktaking. This is normally done by spot-checking a number of items daily so that the complete stockholding may be checked over in, for example, one month. This system saves a considerable amount of time by eliminating full weekly stock checks. The ledger consumption is calculated at standard cost by using a standard order form.

Restaurant checks

The restaurant checks are analysed by dishes served. This may be done by the restaurant cashier if there is one, or by the control

Day	Meat		Fish		Poultry		Fruit/veg.		Groceries		Milk/cream		Bread/cake		Tea/coffee		Sundries	
	Act.	St'd.	Act.	St'd.	Act.	St'd.	Act.	St'd.	Act.	St'd.	Act.	St'd.	Act.	St'd.	Act.	St'd.	Act.	St'd.
Monday	64	66	46	49	24	22	14	12	24	20	10	10	14	18	20	21	3	4
Tuesday	56	55	32	38	28	27	3	4	30	28	9	8	15	14				
Wednesday	48	50	28	28	30	33	18	22	15	15	10	10	16	16				
Thursday	105	110	33	37	15	20	20	26	19	18	9	9	17	17	13	13	2	3
Friday	96	97	40	45	24	28	16	24	24	20	9	9	14	14			1	1
Saturday	48	59	36	44	30	28	15	19	22	21	10	10	14	14	4	3	2	2
Sunday	62	71	28	36	40	42	12	16	23	22	9	9	13	16				
Total	479	508	243	277	191	200	98	123	157	144	66	65	103	109	37	37	8	10
Price variance	+ 29	—	+ 34	—	+ 9	—	+ 25	—	+ 13	—	+ 1	—	+ 6	—	+	—	+ 2	—

Figure 17.4. Purchases summary form

and cashiers daily after meal service. The method is to type the day's menu on the dish analysis form (*Figure 17.6*) and mark off the restaurant checks against them.

Other items to be analysed on similar forms will include:

(*a*) Breakfasts.

(*b*) Early morning coffee/tea.

(*c*) Morning coffee.

(*d*) Sandwiches and biscuits.

(*e*) Bread rolls—gristicks.

(*f*) Afternoon tea.

(*g*) Suppers.

Item: Grapefruit segments A10   St/Price...............   Bin 48......

Supplier: J. Bloggs   *Tel: 82480*   *Order: 36 ; Min. stock: 30*

Date	—	Delivery	Kitchen 1	Kitchen 2	Management	Stores
4/8/69	Stock					42
5/8/69	R 48		3			39
	R 23			2		37
6/8/69	R 56		4			33
	R 27			3		30
7/8/69	R 60				1	29
8/8/69	DN 426	36				65
Consumption			7	5	1	
9/8/69	Stock					65

Figure 17.5. Example of stores ledger form

In fact, every possible food item served should have a corresponding check. Policy decisions must be taken to decide whether detailed items may be counted, for example should vegetables be assessed individually or on average. This also applies to items such as cold sweets.

Dishes served

The dishes served are calculated at dish costs based on portion sizes considered compatible with the market. The daily analyses are

Tuesday 4th November — Lunch									
Dish	Numbers	Total	Code	St/ Price					
Grapefruit cocktail	卌 卌 卌 卌 卌 卌 III	33							
Pâte maison	卌 卌 卌 卌 III	23							
Green pea soup	卌 卌 II	12							
Roast beef	卌 卌 卌 卌 卌 卌 卌 卌 IIII	44							
Kidneys	卌 卌 III	13							
Omelette	卌 卌 I	11							
Vegetables	From main courses	68							
Cold sweets	卌 卌 卌 卌 卌 卌 III	33							
Hot sweets	卌 卌 卌	15							
Coffee	卌 卌 卌 卌 卌 卌 卌	35							
Cheese & biscuits	卌 卌	10							
Total		297							

Figure 17.6. Dish analysis form

summarised weekly (*Figure 17.7*) for posting to the weekly food report.

Staff meals at standard cost

A system of food controls would not be complete if a rational view were not taken of staff feeding costs. Many caterers do not include these in their food cost reports which gives a false impression of the food cost of sales. Some caterers credit an allowance to food purchases which, although providing realistic cost figures, cannot

DISH ANALYSIS SUMMARY									W/E 10/10/69
Item	Code	Mon.	Tues.	Wed.	Thur.	Fri.	Sat.	Sun.	Total
Meat	1								
Fish	2								
Poultry	3								
Fruit, veg.	4								
Groceries	5								
Milk, cream	6								
Bread, cake	7								
Tea, coffee	8								
Sundries	9								
Total									

Figure 17.7. Dish analysis summary form

be treated as accurate. Further, the amount can be used by the chef to cover up inefficient production by reducing the staff meal cost well below the allowance given. By establishing staff feeding dishes and allocating a standard cost to them, the actual cost of staff meals at standard cost may be isolated and the difference from the allowance shown as 'staff feeding variance'.

FOOD REPORT

The information described in the above system culminates in the production of the food report shown in *Figure 17.8*. The object of the document is to indicate action areas.

Item	Code	Opening stock	Purchases	Closing stock	Consump-tion	Staff food	Cost of sales	Cost of meals served	Usage variance	Price variance
Meat	1									
Fish	2									
Poultry	3									
Fruit, veg.	4									
Groceries	5									
Milk, cream	6									
Bread, cake	7									
Tea, coffee	8									
Sundries	9									
Total										

FOOD REPORT   W/E 10/8/69

Staff food allowance
at   × £2·10
    =

	£	%
Food sales		
Gross profit		
Standard gross profit		
Total variance		

	£	%
Usage variance		
Price variance		
Staff food variance		
Menu composition variance		
Total variance		

Figure 17.8. Food report

VARIANCE ANALYSIS

The variances are the key to improved food profitability and should be considered very carefully so that rational decisions can be made, and effective action taken.

Usage variance

This variance will arise under the following circumstances:

(a) *Incorrect receival of goods.* This occurs when suppliers deliver goods of incorrect specifications. For example, poultry which has been specified clean weight may be delivered rough plucked and undrawn.

(b) *Pilferage.* This arises where stock control procedures are slack or adequate security is not exercised in the kitchen.

(c) *Wastage.* Poor preparation or over-production will occur when production has not been carried out to dish specification.

The variances are analysed over food sub-headings so the caterer can trace back to the individuals responsible for preparing that particular item or the supplier who furnished it. Should these two sources not provide apparent reasons for the variance, then stock control and kitchen security procedures should be examined for breakdown.

Price variances

Price variances are easy to isolate by supplier and investigation may be made of relevant orders.

Staff feeding variances

Examination of staff food costs will reveal areas of investigation of under- or over-provision of food.

Menu composition variances

These variances indicate the correctness or otherwise of menu planning. Favourable variances indicate the presentation of items which cannot be considered value for money by the customer. Unfavourable variances indicate bad menu mix and should stimulate study of dish trends to eliminate the variance by presenting an acceptable range of dishes.

Stockholdings

The food report also illustrates stockholdings so that action may be taken to correct the ratio of stock to purchases if necessary.

THE NECESSITY OF COMPLEX CONTROL

Having described what must appear to some caterers a complicated procedure, it is pertinent to consider the relationship of complex control to savings resulting therefrom. Usually, objections to utilising control systems are based on the following points:

- (a) The unit is too small.
- (b) The unit is too large.
- (c) Management is too clever.
- (d) Management is too stupid.
- (e) Costs are too high.
- (f) It involves too much work.

Generally, these opinions are held by those who consider that the 'control costs more than the controlled', and, unfortunately, they may influence other individuals who would probably derive substantial benefit from the institution of such control systems.

In an industry like hotel and catering, where so much can be lost through lack of control, evidence can easily be provided to refute such opinions. For example, a good control clerk will cost £1 000 per annum, but the range of establishments which could benefit from his services in the food operation alone assuming a shortfall of profit of 5% are quite considerable. A shortfall of 5% is, in fact, comparatively low. Normally, an operation producing a gross profit of 57% can usually obtain 65% with control systems. The third column in *Table 17.3* is the gain (or loss) made on the £1 000 per annum investment.

It can be seen that an operation has to be very small not to benefit from £1 000 worth of control. It must also be remembered that the example does not include other departmental savings and cost centres. There may be reasons, however, for not utilising the above system

Table 17.3 Control gain or loss of food operation

Food turnover, £	5% of turnover, £	Gain or loss, £
10 000	500	— 500
15 000	750	— 250
20 000	1 000	Breakeven point
30 000	1 500	+ 500
40 000	2 000	+1 000
50 000	2 500	+1 500
60 000	3 000	+2 000
70 000	3 500	+2 500
80 000	4 000	+3 000
90 000	4 500	+3 500
100 000	5 000	+4 000

and a simpler system may well be employed. Such a system is illustrated below but it should be remembered that it cannot be as
effective as the complex system already described.

STATISTICAL FOOD CONTROL

This system is based upon an analysed 'food inwards book' (*Figure
17.9*) kept by the member of staff responsible for receiving goods.
The weekly totals of the food inwards book reflects the total deliveries
of foodstuffs to the unit. These figures are adjusted for stocks held
and used under the categories shown in the figure. The resulting
adjustment indicates the cost of food consumed by the unit. By
deducting staff feeding costs calculated in the same ratio as the cost
of food consumed for each item bears to the total, the totals in the
food inwards book may be further adjusted.

EXAMPLE

Cost of staff food, £100; cost of consumption, £1 000—analysed in
Table 17.4. The amount consumed per diner relative to the gross
profit can then be calculated. From this information, definite action
may be taken. For example, should the gross profit drop by 5%, the
caterer is looking for cost items aggregating 5% more than he
considers he should spend per diner.

The report (*Figure 17.10*) is fairly straightforward and provides a
ready indication of commodities which are excessive in cost. However, it must be remembered that although it is simple and easy

Date	Supplier	Meat	Poultry	Fish	Fruit, veg.	Groceries	Milk, cream	Bread, cake	Tea, coffee	Sundries

FOOD INWARDS BOOK   W/E 8/10/69

Figure 17.9. Food inwards book form

FOOD REPORT   W/E.............

Item	Meat	Poultry	Fish	Fruit, veg.	Groceries	Milk, cream	Bread, cake	Tea, coffee	Sundries	Total
Stock at start										
Purchases										
Total										
Stock at close										
Consumption										
Staff feeding										
Cost of sales										
Cost per diner										
Budget cost per diner										
Variance per diner										

No. of diners ....

Total diner variance ....

Sales   %

Actual gross profit
less diner variance

Attainable gross profit

Figure 17.10. Food report for statistical control system

Table 17.4 Analysis of cost of food consumption

Item	Cost of consumption, £	%	Staff food, £	Cost of sales, £
Meat	200	20	20	180
Poultry	100	10	10	90
Fish	70	7	7	63
Fruit, veg.	150	15	15	135
Groceries	300	30	30	270
Milk, cream	50	5	5	45
Bread, cake	60	6	6	54
Tea, coffee	40	4	4	36
Sundries	30	3	3	27
Total	£1 000	100	£100	£900

to operate its disadvantage lies in that it is an unsophisticated tool providing comparatively little information.

Direct food cost control

A further simple system of food control is that based on direct costing and is useful for very small operations serving limited, probably permanent, menus or for calculating function food costs.

Dish Analysis												
Items	Mon.	Tues.	Wed.	Thur.	Fri.	Sat.	Total	M	F	P	F, V	Other
Total												

Figure 17.11. Dish analysis form for direct cost food control

A dish analysis (*Figure 17.11*) is made up each day on a batch basis, e.g. no costings are done until the end of a week.

Each dish is costed directly, costs being allocated between prime items, e.g. meat, fish, poultry, fruit and veg., etc. The totals are

Item	Meat	Fish	Poultry	Fruit, veg.	Other	Total
Opening stock Purchases						
Total Closing stock						
Consump- tion Staff food						
Cost of sales Direct costs						
Variance						

	£	%	Remarks
Sales			
Actual gross profit			
Add variance			
Attainable gross profit			

Figure 17.12. Food report for direct cost food control

compared with the costs of the amounts delivered shown in the food inwards book, adjusted for stocks and staff feeding as in the statistical control system. The final report is as shown in *Figure 17.12*.

The three systems of food control illustrated above have been proven in practice and give good results over short periods.

18
Liquor control

As with food, it is relevant also to consider the principles of liquor control so that an understanding may be obtained of the total system before discussing details. This is summarised in *Figure 18.1*.

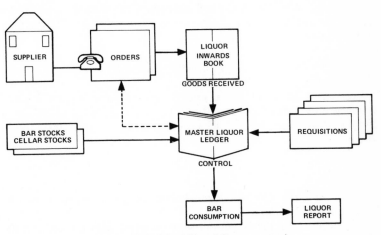

Figure 18.1. Principles of liquor control

From the diagram it can be seen that the whole system is summarised in one master document. the 'master liquor ledger'. The advantage of this is that one source only need be consulted to select many different items of information.

199

ORDERING

The ordering of liquor will be undertaken with reference to the data contained in the master liquor ledger. Each line contained in the ledger will be consulted to see how many lines are below *par stock*. These lines will be ordered according to the *minimum orderable quantities* shown in the ledger. The object of this exercise is to order only those items in such quantities as will be necessary to discharge the current volume of business.

Par stocks

Par stocks are those which it is considered would supply the operation's needs for the period between ordering and delivery (lead time) plus a tolerance to allow for unforeseen emergencies such as van breakdown.

EXAMPLE

The whisky sales for one week average £200 during the summer season for one busy club. If attainable gross profit is 52% then the cost of sales is:

$$\frac{48}{100} \times 200 = £96$$

Lead time is based on a weekly delivery and equals 2 days' delivery plus 7 days' consumption. To this is added a tolerance of 2 days. Therefore, total lead time equals 11 days' consumption at cost:

$$\frac{96}{7} \times 11 = £151$$

If whisky costs £30 per dozen bottles then the par stock will be five cases (60 bottles).

The above example is, of course, concerned with the cellar only. However, par stocks are also allocated to the bars and are usually based upon 3 days' sales at cost.

EXAMPLE

Average bar sales total £700 per week. Then par bar stock at cost is $3/7 \times 700 = £300$. The par bar stock will, of course, be broken down and noted for each line carried. Par stock data are summarised on the master liquor ledger with the relevant line sold.

It should be remembered that because liquor sales volumes normally change radically from summer to winter, par stocks are normally re-calculated for summer and winter seasons.

Minimum orderable quantity

This will be calculated in relation to the par stock and the terms of purchasing. In most cases the minimum orderable quantity will equal the period of consumption at cost. Obviously, occasions arise where large discounts are given to encourage high ordering. This is only feasible provided that the cash tied up in stocks can enjoy a rate higher than the net profit of the unit in relation to capital invested, expressed as a discount on the goods (cash discount). The reason for this is that the cash tied up in stocks cannot be used for the benefit of the business in trading to produce a net profit on capital invested.

EXAMPLE

	£
Capital invested	60 000
Net profit (before depreciation and taxation)	10 000
Return on capital	16·6%

Therefore, any large orders must enjoy a cash discount of more than 16·6% to be acceptable.

When the orders have been assessed they will be written up on a duplicate order book, signed, and the prices noted. The orders will be forwarded to suppliers and the copies passed to the receiving office.

GOODS RECEIVED

When the deliveries are made they will be checked against the duplicate order to ensure that what was actually ordered has arrived. Goods inwards procedure has been dealt with fully in Chapter 6. As has already been mentioned, however, a pertinent criticism made of liquor-receiving procedures is that there is often not enough time to check large loads. A method of dealing with this is to store deliveries in a lockable cage adjacent to the cellar so that the orders may be checked at the storeman's leisure.

Signed delivery notes/invoices will be entered in the liquor inwards book (see Chapter 6) and subsequently passed to the control department weekly with the liquor inwards book.

REQUISITIONS

Liquor requisitions must be made out very carefully to ensure that the following important information is available:

(*a*) Each item is noted by brand name.

(*b*) The exact number is requisitioned.

(*c*) The exact number is actually delivered to the bar.

Requisitions should always be made out in duplicate on an official requisition book and each bar should have its own. In requisitioning, it is important to remember that the barman orders and the cellar delivers. Therefore, the following procedure should be strictly adhered to so that slack practices inviting theft do not take place:

(*a*) The barman should make out the requisition.

(*b*) The cellar should receive the requisition and make up the order.

(*c*) The cellarman should sign a form proving delivery.

(*d*) The order is delivered to the bar.

(*e*) The barman should sign a form proving receipt.

Requisitions are then passed to the control office.

BAR AND CELLAR STOCKS

Bar stocks should be taken regularly, commencing at weekly intervals and possibly extending to monthly intervals. However, it is not advisable to have a longer interval than this. It is preferable also to take all 'broken bottle' stocks in tenths. This method appears to be the most accurate and has no obvious disadvantages. The increase in time involved in stocktaking, as against the conventional method of 32nds, 16ths, 18ths, 20ths, etc., is as much as 30%. Also, since the introduction of decimal currency, calculating cost and selling values have become easier.

The stocks are marked on pre-printed stock forms for subsequent posting to the liquor ledger.

MASTER LIQUOR LEDGER

The ledger is the master document of any liquor system amalgamating the following:

(a) Deliveries.

(b) Requisitions.

(c) Bar stock/cellar stock.

The ledger will be posted weekly. The first stage should be to post only deliveries and requisitions. The resultant balances in the ledger should be equivalent to that held in the cellar, and the cellar stock taken should be checked against them. It is better not to allow bar stocks to be posted in the ledger until the cellar balances are satisfactorily agreed.

The bar stocks should then be posted and, as may be seen from the example below, a bottle consumption for each line by bar may be extracted. In order to trace the possibility of bottles being brought in, all items in the system are recorded by brand name, *not* as general headings such as gin, whisky, vodka, etc.

Bar consumption

The bar consumption figures are copied on to pre-printed sheets known as 'bar consumption sheets' from which consumption at cost and selling price may be calculated.

Liquor report

The report for each bar will be made showing each group of lines, e.g. whisky, gin, brandy, etc. The following items will also be included in the report so that the totals may be adjusted to reflect the gross profit on items sold only:

(a) *Ullage.* Bar credit checks.

(b) *Special price differences.* Amount not received due to price decrease.

(c) *Entertaining.* Management drinks recorded on bar credit checks at selling price.

(d) *Off-sales.* Price differences only.

SUPPLEMENTARY CONTROLS

Bottle-for-bottle requisitioning

To avoid bars becoming overstocked or rising above par stock-holding, caterers often insist that requisitions may only be made when an empty bottle may be exchanged for a full one.

An advantage of this system is that daily stock control against cash received may be carried out fairly quickly, if necessary, by becoming familiar with the par stockholding and calculating the difference, i.e. stock sold.

Marked bottles

Many caterers mark bottles with a stamp which cannot be easily duplicated, usually a signature, so that foreign bottles may be easily identified. The procedure is, however, absolutely worthless if the bottles are not smashed or the labels obliterated.

Other methods in use have considerable disadvantages over the system described above. In some cases, even systems that are well known and well used do not reveal any meaningful information.

FRAUDS

This chapter would not be complete without reference to frauds and some of these are outlined below.

Watering

Spirit watering may take place in the bar or the cellar and is not so rare as is commonly thought. Obviously, the bar is the easiest place to water spirits and for that reason a hydrometer should be used on random occasions during stocktakes. It is always advisable to rotate stock in the cellar and examine cellar stock for damaged seals.

Checks

Checks may be charged with drinks not taken, the excess being taken in cash or stock. Management checks are prone to this and for that reason all management drink checks should be signed at the time they are incurred.

Foreign liquor

As referred to above, the bringing in and selling in the bar of foreign liquor, with the resulting pocketing of cash, is a fairly common fraud. It can be eliminated by marking bottles and operating a par stock and bottle-for-bottle requisition system.

Cash control

Many small frauds are committed by under-ringing or not ringing up the till at all, and the best method of dealing with this is to place the till in clear view of the customers. The till should also be equipped with a 'locked-in' tally roll, so that each transaction may be recorded and the total balanced against the cash taken. All credit drinks should be paid for through the normal front-office accounting system, as only front-office receipts are proof of payment.

The following case example includes consideration of the beverage control problems of a medium-sized hotel.

CASE EXAMPLE: MANAGEMENT AUDIT, NONESUCH HOTEL

Introduction

This report was commissioned by Mr. Ay, managing director of the *Nonesuch Hotel*, Notown. It was agreed that Mr. David A. Fearn should carry out a management audit of the hotel.

Terms of reference

The following terms of reference were stipulated by Mr. Ay:

(*a*) Particular attention should be paid to the accounting and control procedures; (*b*) Effectiveness of the management team should be considered, with reference to its function during the next decade; (*c*) Consideration of the economic potential of the *Nonesuch Hotel*.

Method of operating

The management team of the hotel was interviewed extensively throughout the first day of the audit and pertinent comments investigated in detail. The personnel interviewed were:

Mr. Ay	Managing director
Mr. Bee	Manager
Mr. Cee	Secretary
Mr. Dee	Assistant manager

The accounts for the previous three financial years were examined and converted to a departmental system of hotel accounts so that comparison with other hotels' performance could be made. The rate of profitability was considered in relation to turnover level, and standards of products and service.

Economic function

The hotel's main business objective is to cater for foreign tourists during the summer months May to September. The hotel also accommodates courses run by firms of consultants and industrial companies.

The addition of the new wing during the last nine years to cater for the plentiful tourist trade obliged the hotel to consider marketing strategies to attract guests during the winter. These strategies manifested themselves as the creation of cultural activities such as 'teach-ins' in various subjects including antiques and music, to attract winter guests, and the provision of a conference room as part of the new wing.

Examination of the priority of the business objectives indicated that the course business was not exploited fully, whilst the 'teach-ins' were not as profitable as either of the other business objectives.

COMPETITION

The hotel has no peers currently in Noshire in the tourist market. However, it is suspected that the proposed *Notown Hilton* will provide considerable competition for all the markets that the *Nonesuch Hotel* currently enjoys.

Conference hotels within approximate reach of London have, in recent years, modernised their facilities considerably in anticipation of the rapidly increasing course and conference market. Others are attempting to enter the field and currently the *Nonesuch Hotel* considers the following hotels as direct competitors, amongst others:

....

....

Studies of the marketing effect of hotels with course facilities indicates a high demand, as those hotels which adequately promote

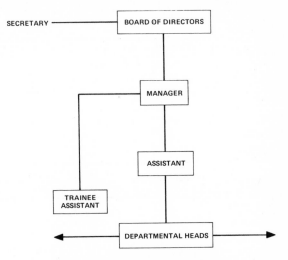

Figure 18.2. The company structure

such facilities tend to enjoy high room occupancy after comparatively short promotional campaigns.

Company structure

Figure 18.2 shows the company structure. It is observed that the manager has the following departmental heads reporting to him:

Assistant manager	Head porter
Trainee assistant	Housekeeper
Reservations manager	Maintenance
Head waiter	Chef
Bar and cellar	

and that he is directly responsible for all departments of the hotel. The assistant manager covers the manager's duties but has few responsibilities apart from some clerical duties.

Unit: Nonesuch Hotel							Accounting period no.:				

Department	No.	Net sales £	%	Direct materials £	%	Gross margin £	%	Wages & staff costs £	%	Net margin £
Accommodation	1	100 326		—	—	100 326	100	22 528	23	77 798
Food	2	91 116		40 297	44	50 819	56	27 878	31	22 941
Liquor	2	54 136		35 918	66	18 218	34	3 638	7	14 580
Other operated depts.	3									
Total		£245 578		£76 215	31	£169 363	69	£54 044	22	£115 319
Other income	4	3 426		313		3 113		—	—	3 113
Administration	5							7 900		
Advertising	6									
Heat, light, power	7									
General	8							3 019		
Total	9	£3 426		£313		£3 113		£10 919		£3 113
Hotel control level	10	249 004		76 528	32	172 476	68	64 963	24	107 513
Rent, rates, insurance	11									
Other additions/deduc.	12							7 862		
Depreciation	13									
Repairs & maintenance	14							3 641		
Other activities	15	396		—		396				396
Total		£396		—		£396		£11 503		£396
Net profit		£249 400		£76 528	32	£172 872	68	£76 466	30	£96 406

Figure 18.3. Accounts for Nonesuch Hotel

		From:				Actual		To:			
ed s	%	Profit — Loss £	%	4-Week budget £	%	cumu- lative £	%	Budget cumu- lative £	%	Variance £	%
417	4	73 381	73			76 381	76			3 000	3
988	8	14 953	17			19 363	22			4 410	5
	—	14 580	27			17 775	33			3 195	6
405	5	£102 914	42			£113 519	46			£10 605	4
	—	3 113	1			3 113	1			—	—
		106 027	43			116 632	47			10 605	4
900		16 800	7			19 255	8			(2 455)	(1)
455		2 455	1			2 455	1			—	—
935		9 935	4			7 480	3			2 455	1
026		10 045	4			10 045	4			—	—
316		£39 235	16			£39 235	16			—	—
721	17	66 792	27			77 397	31			10 605	4
457		7 457	3			7 457	3				
843		10 705	6			10 705	6				
057		5 057	2			5 057	2				
382		20 023	8			17 568	7			2 455	
391		1 995	—			1 995	—				
130		£45 237	19			£42 782	18			£2 455	
851	30	£21 555	8			£34 615	13			£13 060	

There does not appear to be any provision for formal consultation with the managing director, discussions taking place when casual meetings occur from day to day. Management–staff meetings are not held, having been allowed to lapse.

Health of earnings

The set of accounts is shown in *Figure 18.3.*

CALCULATION OF NET PROFIT FOR HOTEL COMPARISON

	£	
Net profit as per accounts	21 555	(appended)
Add insurance	3 233	
Net profit as per audited accounts	24 788	

PROFIT EFFECTIVENESS

Profit effectiveness is shown in *Table 18.1.*

Table 18.1 Profit effectiveness

Item	1968, £	1967, £	1966, £
Net profit	21 555	25 963	21 262
Add. repairs	20 023	12 784	11 438
Total	41 578	38 747	32 700
Less repairs at 7%	17 185	13 223	11 662
Net profit I.H.C.*	24 393	25 524	21 038

* Inter-hotel comparison.

Table 18.2 shows the net profit as percentage of sales.

Table 18.2 Net profit as a percentage of sales

Item	1968 £	1968 %	1967 £	1967 %	1966 £	1966 %
Sales	249 000	100	188 906	100	166 618	100
Net profit	24 393	9	25 524	12	21 038	12·6

NET PROFIT AS A PERCENTAGE OF CAPITAL INVESTED

Net profit as percentage of capital invested is shown in *Table 18.3.*

Table 18.3 Net profit as percentage of capital invested

Item	1968 £	1968 %	1967 £	1967 %	1966 £	1966 %
Total as per a/cs.	334 626		217 055		185 325	
Less dep. w/o	51 202		46 895		43 198	
Fixed assets	283 424		170 160		142 127	
Return		7·9		15		14·8

PROFIT SHORTFALL, 1968

It is considered that the *Nonesuch Hotel* should generate a profit of between 12 and 16% of sales on current turnover, i.e. £33 715–£40 825 to return 10–15% on current capital investment before taxation. This would indicate a rate of return on capital after taxation of 7–11%, which must be the minimum acceptable target to the hotel's management.

PROFIT AS PER 1968 ACCOUNTS

In *Table 18.4* the profit as per the 1968 accounts is shown.

SERVICE AND GOODS EFFICIENCY

Tables 18.5 and *18.6* show the service and goods efficiency. The breakeven record shows that sales generated to 1967 of £22 288 generated only £4 486 marginal profit (20%), and sales to 1968 were surpassed by costs to the amount of £1 131. If the break-even rate does not improve, the current deficit of working capital will worsen and permanent capital will be required should cash flow difficulties be avoided.

Control systems

The control systems of the hotel are inadequate and contribute to the gross margin deficits of food and liquor prime costs.

Table 18.4 Profit as per 1968 accounts

Item	Variance cost £	%	Profit Minimum £	%	Maximum £	%
Add unfavourable variances			21 555	8	21 555	8
Accommodation, wages	3 000	3				
Food cost	3 510–8 200	4–9				
Liquor cost	5 900–8 000	11–16				
Heat, light, power	2 455					
Rates and maintenance	2 455					
Total	£17 320–£24 110 ──────→		17 320	6	24 110	10
			38 875	14	45 665	18
Deduct unfavourable variances						
Higher wages	2 455	5				
Admin. wages	2 705					
Total	£5 160 ──────→		5 160	2	5 160	2
			£33 715	12	£50 825	16

Table 18.5 Breakeven record 1966–68

Item	1966	%	1967	%	1968	%
Sales, £	166 168	100	188 906	100	249 400	100
Breakeven, £	145 580		163 382		225 007	91
Net profit, £	21 038	12·6	25 524	12	24 393	9

Table 18.6 Sales, costs and profit 1966–68

Year	Sales, £	Costs, £	Profit, £
1966	166 168	145 580	21 038
	+22 288	+17 802	+4 486
1967	188 906	163 382	25 524
	+ 60 494	+ 61 625	+(1 131)
1968	249 400	225 007	24 393

FOOD CONTROL

There are two independent systems of food control operated in the hotel, neither of which gives correct results. The records kept by Mr. Cee are not corrected for stocks and consequently show considerable monthly fluctuation. The system maintained by Mr. Ee does not include all food purchases and tends to show higher gross margin results than are actually achieved.

LIQUOR CONTROL

The liquor system is confined to bin cards, bar stocks being taken and calculated by an outside firm of stocktakers. The bin cards are unsatisfactory as they have not been changed for five years; the cellarman erases the information at the top of the card and starts again. Neither system is sophisticated enough to control adequately the sales of food and liquor of the volume which the hotel enjoys.

SALOON BAR

It is understood that the saloon bar has been let for £2 000 per annum. Should the takings of the bar be in excess of £150 per week it is recommended that this policy be reconsidered.

Financial policies

No person is responsible for financial planning, budgetary control or target setting. Mr. Ay has adopted this responsibility but he is also involved in marketing, day-to-day management and other duties which necessarily precludes him from detailed work.

There are no financial reports to indicate to top management deviations from the management objectives expected of each product and operation.

STOCK TURN

The rate of stock turned round over the years 1966–1968 is as shown in *Table 18.7*.

The rate of stock turned is far lower than would normally be expected. Should the stock be turned at an efficient rate, i.e. 10 times per annum for liquor and 36 times per annum for food, the amounts shown in *Table 18.9* could be contributed to bank, and so reduce the adverse working capital ratio.

It is noticed that food stockholding improved considerably in the period 1966–1967. However, both food and liquor stocks are too

Table 18.7 Rate of stock turn-round

Item	1966, %	1967, %	1968, %	Considered good, %
Liquor	3·7	4·0	3·9	9–10
Food	10·3	27·4	23·6	36–42

high, and are being very expensively financed, interest alone being in the region of £500 per annum.

WORKING CAPITAL

The working capital ratios are shown in *Table 18.8* for the years 1966–1968.

Table 18.8 Working capital ratios

Item	1966	1967	1968
Assets, £	26 065	20 494	31 364
Liabilities, £	61 491	65 245	80 455
Deficit, £	35 426	44 751	49 091
		+9 325	+4 340

The working capital ratio is worsening dramatically annually and may only be corrected by an influx of permanent capital or increased profitability. Current profits cannot contribute materially to the working capital deficit, although a reduction in stockholding of £6 200 and achievement of profit effectiveness to increase profits after taxation, dividends, etc., by £5 200 would achieve balance of working capital in eight or nine years, as follows:

	£
Present deficit of working capital	49 091
less excess stockholding	6 200
	42 891
9 × £5 200	46 800
Excess of working capital	£3 909

Table 18.9 Improved food and liquor stockholding

Item	1966 Food, £	1966 Liquor, £	1967 Food, £	1967 Liquor, £	1968 Food, £	1968 Liquor, £
Cost of sales	43 534	32 864	44 852	35 691	49 747	35 918
Stock turn	×36	×10	×36	×10	×36	×10
Stock held	1 206	3 286	1 220	3 569	1 390	3 592
Stock actually held	4 102	8 548	1 636	9 357	2 107	9 187
Contribution to working capital	2 896	5 262	416	5 788	617	5 595
Total	£8 158		£6 204		£6 212	

Management effectiveness

BOARD OF DIRECTORS

The management of the hotel consists of the board of directors, Mr. Ay, Mr. Ef and Mr. Gee. Mr. Ay is the only executive director and regular board meetings are infrequent and are not held upon a formal basis.

To strengthen the board it has been suggested that Mr. Bee joins the board or some other who would assume the post of managing director. A fifth member would be co-opted from outside the hotel.

LINE MANAGEMENT

From interviews with line management, it was found that considerable difficulties existed for management in the following respects:

(*a*) The hours worked are generally excessive and proper programming of duties and departmentalisation of management duties would obviate this.

(*b*) The manager has all departmental heads reporting to him.

The management team require considerably more knowledge of business ideas and techniques. There is currently little understanding of business principles and objectives.

It is evident that the manager has some thoughts in this direction as he expressed interest in the following: daily sales report; budgetary control; and food cost control.

Management incentives

There is an existing incentive scheme based upon winter turnover payable to the manager.

Recommendations

Principal recommendations are that:

(*a*) Course and conference business should be exploited more fully by arranging campaigns directed towards the 'Times Top 500 Companies', firms of management consultants, and professional institutions. This should be supplemented by follow-up visits by Mr. Ay or Mr. Bee.

(*b*) Because the volume of sales shows a considerable bias towards food and liquor, it is recommended that the management structure should be departmentalised to exploit food and beverage control opportunities, as shown in *Figure 18.4.* This organisation structure consists of a logical chain of command which will enable management to administer more rationally.

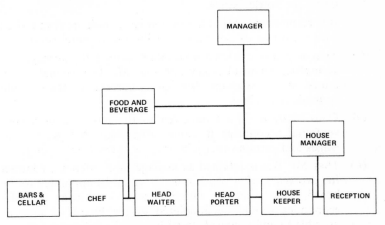

Figure 18.4. Management structure departmentalisation

(*c*) That regular meetings should be held by management with Mr. Ay to ensure that deviations from planned performance are corrected.

(*d*) Management and departmental head meetings should be held frequently for the following reasons:

(*i*) To inform the staff of the hotel's performance.

(*ii*) To settle inter-departmental disputes.

(*iii*) To consider forward business arrangements.

(*iv*) To discuss matters of welfare.

(*v*) To consider suggestions.

It will be found that such meetings increase enthusiasm and interest.

(*e*) A system of monthly management accounts and target setting should be installed in the hotel to produce management information for timely decision-taking. The accounts should be presented in the departmentalised form shown above. The system would be allied to management and departmental objectives.

(*f*) It is recommended that a system of food control should be installed to rationalise the food costs of the hotel. A suitable system for this purpose would be standard food cost control.

(*g*) That the hotel assumes responsibility for its liquor stock-taking records, and these should be controlled through a system of cellar and bar control based upon par stocks and bottle-for-bottle issues.

(*h*) It is recommended that the saloon bar should be reappraised with regard to its potential contribution to hotel profits.

(*i*) That a young qualified accountant should be employed to administer financial policy and that Mr. Gee should be retained as his assistant. Mr. Gee's current assistant would be made redundant.

(*j*) Consideration should be given to the purchase of a conventional accounting machine rather than N.C.R. so that wages and certain other jobs may be carried out upon it.

(*k*) That Mr. Bee is retained as manager and offered a contract for two years, after which time he would be appointed to the board. That someone with a proven knowledge of hotel economics should be appointed to the board as soon as possible to add financial strength.

(*l*) That Mr. Dee is appointed food and beverage manager and Mr. Ee be substituted by a higher calibre man for the post of house manager.

(*m*) That job specifications are established for management and departmental heads with a view to programming work done and allowing adequate off-duty periods.

(*n*) That a development programme is arranged for the line managers in conjunction with themselves and the hotel.

(*o*) That management incentives should be paid upon departmental responsibilities on net profit, as follows:

    (*i*) Manager.   Hotel net profit, 5% over £30 000.

    (*ii*) Food and beverage. Food dept., 5% over £20 000.
                                 Liquor dept., 5% over £20 000.

    (*iii*) House.   Accommodation, 5% over £80 000.

    (*iv*) Chef.   £1 per week per 1% over 60%.

    (*v*) Barman.   £3 per 1% surplus per month.

The existing incentive schemes should be stopped in favour of the above.

Assignment: food and beverage systems installation, Nonesuch Hotel

SUMMARY OF DATA—MANAGEMENT AUDIT

(a) Appointment of food and beverage manager.

(b) A food gross profit shortfall of £3 510 to £8 200 dependent upon quality of raw materials and portion sizes. Current quality and portion sizes indicate a potential saving of £8 200. However, a necessary improvement in food quality and portions should provide a saving of £3 510.

(c) Stocks of food and beverages are excessive and should be reduced by £617 and £5 595, respectively.

(d) A liquor gross profit of 34% (this includes tobacco gross profit) which should be in the region of £5 900 based upon the current price structure. An increase in prices as has been recommended would provide additional liquor gross profit of £8 000.

(e) The ratio of liquor sales to total sales is low. In an operation of this nature liquor sales should be over 75% of food sales. The present situation is caused by the location and nature of bar service.

(f) Liquor wages are lower than would normally be expected in an operation of this kind, the shortfall being in the region of £2 455.

ASSIGNMENT OBJECTIVES (ANNUAL)

(a) To increase food gross profit to 65% (after deducting the cost of staff meals), e.g. by £3 510.

(b) To increase liquor gross profit to 51%, i.e. by £8 000.

(c) To increase liquor wages to provide a full and effective service, i.e. by £2 455.

(d) Improvement of food quality, service and preparation.

(e) Decrease of stockholdings by £617 and £5 595 for food and beverages, respectively.

FOOD CONTROL—21 DAYS

Principles of system outlined to food and beverage manager—1 day

The senior assistant manager was appointed to the position of food and beverage manager. In order to familiarise him with the new systems to be installed, he was to work in close conjunction with the consultants during the period of the assignment. An induction period of one day was planned to completely familiarise him with the principles of the system.

Food staff teach-in—1 day

A teach-in was organised for all the staff working in the food operation early in the assignment to illustrate the system to them in simple terms.

Examination of current raw materials and menus—3 days

Food and beverage consultants examined the present raw material supplies and extracted a list of all products used together with standard prices of those goods. This information was compiled into standard order forms.

Menus were examined carefully in conjunction with the chef and management; from this examination standard dish cards were produced for every item produced by the hotel.

Initial stocktaking and commencement of stock ledger—3 days

The standard order forms were used for stocktaking and the method of calculation shown to control staff. The initial stock of dry goods, by number and weight, was used to commence the dry stores stock ledger.

Check analysis and requisitions—4 days

A teach-in, lasting one day, was held to illustrate to all restaurant staff and cashiers how restaurant checks should be written out and how they should be analysed.

The cashiers' check analysis system was subsequently installed over three days to produce daily 'food sales analyses' by items served. The method of writing out requisitions and the procedure of requisitioning was also illustrated and subsequently installed.

Use of standard order forms—3 days

Both the chef and storeman were instructed in the use of standard order forms for purchasing and the procedure to be followed in using them. This procedure was monitored for five days.

Staff feeding—1 day

The food and beverage manager and chef produced a schedule of staff meals which could be used for daily staff food-costing purposes. The schedules were put into daily operation.

Compilation of data—5 days

The incoming data were analysed and compiled into the food report. This exercise was monitored for three weeks until control staff became fully familiarised with the procedure. A meeting was held with management subsequent to each report to discuss and decide action to be taken.

LIQUOR CONTROL—TOTAL TIME 16 DAYS

Principles of system—1 day

The food and beverage manager spent one day with the consultants to completely familiarise him with the principles of the system.

Liquor staff teach-in—1 day

A teach-in was organised for all staff involved in the liquor operation at the commencement of the assignment so that the system could be explained in simple terms.

Initial stocktaking—4 days

The consultants in conjunction with the hotel staff spent one day establishing an opening stock of every beverage item in the hotel. From these stock records the following data were formulated:

(a) Master liquor ledger. This contains a record of the movement of all lines by outlet (1 day).

(b) Par stock schedule. This is the calculation of minimum stockholdings to be held in the bars and cellar (1 day).

(c) Stocktaking forms (1 day).

Negotiation of prices and suppliers—3 days

Consideration was made of the volume of all items sold in relation to the amount of stock held of each line in the hotel. Returned stock lists were compiled of:

(a) All stock held over par.

(b) Discarded lines.

The amount of stock shown was returned to the relevant suppliers. This took two days.

During the third day, the consumption of all lines was forecast and suppliers asked to quote terms thereon. A supplier was selected who could discharge the requirements of the hotel regarding delivery and terms.

Second stocktaking—1 day

A second stocktaking took place using the forms produced which decreased stocktaking time by 50% to two hours.

Writing-up of master liquor ledger—2 days

The hotel staff were carefully instructed in the method of writing up the liquor ledger and extracting balances of consumption per item by outlet. Cellar balances were checked against the ledger balances and variances investigated. Par stocks were checked and variances from par stock levels investigated. Liquor stock consumption was calculated and the gross profit and surplus for each outlet investigated.

Teach-in—1 day

A teach-in was held for liquor staff to illustrate the correct method of dealing with requisitions, deliveries and checks.

Sales mix—1 day

The sales mix of beverages was considered carefully to isolate losses due to price and product mix. New beverage and wine lists were produced to achieve the desired gross profit.

Measures and outage—½ day

Bar staff were interviewed and the correct measures for each item assessed and corrected where out of line.

Monitoring—1½ days

The system was monitored for three weeks to ensure that it was operating adequately, any deviations being corrected immediately.

BONUS SYSTEMS—TOTAL TIME 2 DAYS

Incorporated with the systems discussed above were bonus systems for bar and food staff.

Food bonus system—1 day

The bonus system for food was based upon food cost of sales and was applicable to the chef. The system had a two-fold effect:

(a) To encourage a profit of 65% of sales.
(b) To discourage profits of over 65% of sales.

The system was assessed upon a maximum weekly increase of £5. It came into being at 61% gross profit and operated to 69%, maximum bonus being paid at 65% as follows:

61% + £1	66% + £4
62% + £2	67% + £3
63% + £3	68% + £2
64% + £4	69% + £1
65% + £5	70% − (zero)

Liquor bonus system—1 day

The liquor bonus was paid to the barman on the basis of surplus and was designed to take advantage of natural surpluses, but to discourage short measures. The bonuses were different for bars with differing sales mix. For example:

	Cocktail bar		Dispense bar
Surplus	1% + £1	Surplus	$\frac{1}{2}$% + £1
	2% + £2		1% + £2
	3% + £3		1$\frac{1}{2}$% + £3
	4% + £4		2% + £4
	5% + £5		2$\frac{1}{2}$% + £5

The bonuses above were not the only bonuses awarded in the hotel. However, other bonuses are not relevant to the above and have not been recorded here.

FOOD QUALITY SERVICE AND PREPARATION—10 DAYS

The improvement of the above items was undertaken through intensive training and discussion. However, one technique used may be found to be of some assistance to other caterers.

The chef was encouraged to produce one *à la carte* dish each day for table d'hôte lunch and dinner sessions. Very clear specifications for these dishes was given by the consultants and food and beverage manager and the dishes had to be produced in accordance with these specifications. A colour photograph was taken of each dish and a copy retained by the chef and food and beverage manager. The photographs provided a means of quality control to maintain the desired standard of cuisine and presentation.

TOTAL CONSULTANCY ASSIGNMENT— 49 DAYS

The assignment achieved its targets within 3 months providing an improvement in net profitability of £6 000 in 6 months (approximately twice the amount of the consultancy fee).

19
Manpower control

The control of wages is of utmost importance to the caterer. As may be seen from the numerous examples of accounts produced in this book, wages payments are in the region of 30% of all income. The payroll and burden consists of a number of items as follows:

(a) *Gross wages.*   The rate for the job.
(b) *NHI and (formerly) SET.* Compulsory state payroll taxes.
(c) *Graduated pension.*   Compulsory state pension.
(d) *Staff feeding.*   From 12½p to 50p per day per head.
(e) *Staff accommodation.* From £375 to £750 per annum per head.

Apart from obvious high wage costs of an operation it is important to consider the costs of employing new personnel, as shown in *Table 19.1*.

Table 19.1 Cost of employing new personnel

Factor	Commis waiter, £	General manager, £
Cost of advertisement (agency commission)	10	500
Cost of interviewing and selection	10	50
Cost of first week's salary (ineffective)	10	60
Total	£30	£610

Many authorities consider that the cost of employing management personnel is in the region of £1 000 per head. However, a figure of £1 500 per head would be considered an average cost to an average hotel.

EXAMPLE

A hotel employing 100 staff has a turnover of 250% (not unusual). The hotel has, therefore, 250 new staff per annum. Each new member of staff costs £30 to employ. Consequently, the annual cost of new employment is £7 500 at least.

Obviously, the most direct method of reducing costs in this area is to ensure good staff relations and formulate a labour strategy which works. It is also important to know when labour turnover is getting out of line and the wages report shown in Chapter 16 indicates when this is occurring. It is the responsibility of management to investigate variances from expected staff turnover and to take action to eliminate the situation causing such variances.

DEPARTMENTAL WAGES

Food and liquor departments

One of the most simple and effective methods of wage assessment is departmental assessment in relation to departmental sales, shown in *Tables 19.2* and *19.3*, with regard to the food and liquor departments, respectively. It can be seen that wages must not exceed 30% if a reasonable profit is to be earned.

Other departments

Other departmental wage ratios are struck by considering their ratio in comparison to total sales (*Table 19.5*).

The percentages will only apply to annual results. Therefore, an essential aid to wages control is budgetary control upon a monthly, four-weekly or weekly basis.

The payroll as above is broken down into control periods in terms of cash, as indicated in *Table 19.4* for the food department. The caterer can then see that he can keep his wage cost within reasonable monthly limits as a ratio for sales.

Table 19.2 Food departmental assessment in relation to sales

Sales £	Cost of sales £	%	Gross margin £	%	Wages £	%	Net margin £	%	Dept. costs £	%	Dept. profit £	%
100 000	35 000	35	65 000	65	25 000	25	40 000	40	15 000	15	25 000	25

Table 19.3 Liquor departmental assessment in relation to sales

Sales £	Cost of sales £	%	Gross margin £	%	Wages £	%	Net margin £	%	Dept. costs £	%	Dept. profit £	%
50 000	25 000	50	25 000	50	6 500	13	18 500	37	1 000	2	17 500	35

Table 19.4 Food department cash control periods

Item	Jan.	Feb.	March	April	May	June	July	Aug.	Sept.	Oct.	Nov.	Dec.	Total
Sales, £	3 000	5 000	8 000	9 000	10 000	11 000	12 000	12 000	11 000	8 000	5 000	6 000	100 000
Wages, £	2 092	2 092	2 092	2 092	2 092	2 092	2 092	2 092	2 092	2 092	2 092	2 092	25 000
%	70	42	26	23	21	19	17	17	19	26	42	35	25

Table 19.5 Wage ratio comparison to total sales

Item	£	%	Remarks
Total sales	150 000	100	
Admin. wages	7 500	5	Average is from 3 to 8% dependent upon management strength required
Heat, light, power	750	0·5	
Other additions and deductions	2 250	1·5	Directors' fees
Repairs and maintenance	750	0·5	
Sub-total	7 500	7·5	
Food	25 000	16·7	
Liquor	6 500	4·3	
Total wages	£43 000	28·5	

MANPOWER COST ELEMENTS

Caterers are becoming interested in more sophisticated methods of measuring wage costs and are considering industrial methods of cost control. One such method of measuring cost is by isolating the main function of the job and allocating a cost based upon the effective operation of that job.

Standard cost of service per cover	17½p
Covers served 7 days ended 4.1.72	840
Standard cost of service 840 × 17½p	£147
Actual service wages paid	£170
Unfavourable wages variance	£33

The variance is equivalent to the wages of two men during the week and indicates quickly to management that action should be taken to reduce the amount.

Obviously, restaurateurs can never be certain (except on a Saturday night) how much trade they are likely to enjoy and, therefore, cannot reduce and increase staff in accordance with the business. Consequently, more subtle methods of reducing service cost should be considered, such as transferring staff to other work, e.g. decorating, expansion, etc. It is known that some hotels have carried out their maintenance programmes at very low cost by adopting these ideas, and it is certain that there are many necessary jobs that could be undertaken by staff not gainfully employed in other departments.

Kitchen wage costs are considered in a slightly different and more complex manner. The reason for this is that many different jobs are carried out which take varying amounts of time. The system is based upon the cost cards used in food cost control (see Chapter 17). The cards (*Figure 19.1*) also contain standard labour costs per

Labour costs	Dish name
Portions	
1 —	
10 —	
20 —	
30 —	
40 —	
50 —	
100 —	

Figure 19.1. Dish labour costs card

dish which are compiled in the same way as food costs. From the card a total kitchen standard labour cost can be isolated which may

Department	Actual	Standard	Variance
Veg. prep.			
Fish			
Larder			
Pâtisserie			
Still room			
Plate room			
Potwash			
Total			

Figure 19.2. Departmental total wages cost card

230

Food operation cost analysis				W/E:		
Item	Price variance	Usage variance	Total food variance	Labour variance analysis		
Meat				Veg. prep.		
Fish				Fish		
Poultry				Larder		
Fruit, veg.				Pâtisserie		
Groceries				Still room		
Milk, cream				Plate room		
Tea, coffee				Potwash		
Bread, cake						
Sundries						
Sub-total						
Staff feeding variance						
Menu composition variance				Restaurant		
Total food variance				Total labour variance		
					Expected	Actual
Food variance				Average food check		
Labour variance				Diners this week		
Total variance				Diners to date		
Remarks						
				Food and beverage manager		

Figure 19.3. Variance analysis record

be measured against actual labour cost. Obviously, a persistent variance must be isolated so that the kitchen can be reorganised to eliminate it.

The provision of reasonably priced electronic accounting equipment and small computers allows an easy and rapid method of providing more detailed information. The total wages cost can be analysed departmentally, as shown in *Figure 19.2*.

VARIANCE ANALYSIS

The production of standard cost analysis for the whole food operation allows sophisticated variance analysis to be undertaken by catering management. A variance analysis record is shown in *Figure 19.3*.

20

Total control and management action

SCALES OF CATERING IN RELATION TO TOTAL CONTROL

The concern of this chapter is to show how the individual control systems discussed so far can be combined to provide the hotelier or caterer with total control. Varying degrees of control are required by different scales of catering, and, in order to indicate this, these scales have been grouped under the following headings:

(a) Café, fish and chip shop or snack bar.

(b) Public house with catering.

(c) Popular restaurants and small hotel restaurants.

(d) Medium-class restaurants (B and C markets).

(e) Motorway catering.

(f) Haute cuisine restaurant.

(g) Hotel restaurant

(h) High-volume restaurants.

(i) Multi-restaurant complex and chain operations.

Café, fish and chip shop or snack bar

Very simple control information would be used derived from invoices, wage sheet and till roll, as shown in *Table 20.1*. Stocks will probably be so low that stocktaking is hardly necessary. These operations are normally small enough to control by watching the percentages shown.

Public house with catering

The short form account shown in *Table 20.1* can be adjusted as follows to include the liquor operation (*Table 20.2*). Because the same staff usually operate the food and liquor operations, the wages

Table 20.1 Control information required for café, fish and chip shop or snack bar

Items	£	%
Sales	50 000	100
Cost	20 000	40
Gross margin	30 000	60
Wages and burden	12 500	25
Net margin	17 500	35
Other costs	7 500	15
Net profit	10 000	20

are shown as one figure. The information for the account will be obtained from food invoices, till rolls, invoices and wage sheets.

The amount of liquor sold by the operation demands that an accurate stocktaking system on a *simple* basis should be installed,

Table 20.2 Cost control information for public house with catering

Item	£	%
Sales		
Food	10 000	100
Liquor	30 000	100
Total	£40 000	100
Costs		
Food	5 000	50
Liquor	21 000	70
Total	£26 000	65
Gross margin	14 000	35
Wages	8 000	20
Net margin	6 000	15
Other costs	3 000	7·5
Net profit	£3 000	7·5

as shown in *Figure 20.1*. However, because the food sales are comparatively low it is unlikely that any sophisticated food stocktaking system should be used.

Item	Opening stock	Purchases	Total	Closing stock	Liquor consumed	Allowances, £	C/P, £	S/P, £	At cost, £	At selling, £
J. Walker	$4\frac{5}{10}$	12	$16\frac{5}{10}$	$5\frac{4}{10}$	$11\frac{1}{10}$	9·60	2·60	4·40	28·60	51·48
J. and B.	$2\frac{1}{10}$	6	$8\frac{1}{10}$	4	$4\frac{1}{10}$		2·60	4·40	10·66	18·04
Haig	$1\frac{3}{10}$	6	$7\frac{3}{10}$	$2\frac{2}{10}$	$5\frac{1}{10}$		2·60	4·40	13·26	22·44
Teachers	$2\frac{4}{10}$	12	$14\frac{4}{10}$	$4\frac{3}{10}$	$10\frac{1}{10}$		2·60	4·40	26·26	44·44
Black & White	$1\frac{3}{10}$	6	$7\frac{3}{10}$	$3\frac{2}{10}$	$4\frac{1}{10}$		2·60	4·40	10·66	18·54
Gordons	$6\frac{2}{10}$	24	$30\frac{2}{10}$	$8\frac{1}{10}$	$22\frac{1}{10}$	4·20	2·50	4·40	55·25	97·24
Booths	$2\frac{1}{10}$	12	$14\frac{1}{10}$	$4\frac{1}{10}$	10		2·50	4·40	25·00	44·00

Figure 20.1. Simple liquor stock form

Popular restaurants and small hotel restaurants

Most popular restaurants tend to be chain operations. However, for the benefit of the few individual operations, the control aspect is discussed here. As similar forms are used for small unlicensed hotels they have also been discussed in this section.

Operations such as these will probably make up their accounts from a 'goods inward book', stock-takes, sales summary, petty cash book and wages sheets, as shown in *Table 20.3*.

Table 20.3 Cost control information for popular restaurants and small hotel restaurants

Item	Actual this period		Budget this period	
	£	%	£	%
Sales				
Rooms*	5 000	100	4 800	100
Food	6 000	100	6 200	100
Total	£11 000	100	£11 000	100
Costs				
Food	2 400	40†	2 604	42†
Gross margin	8 600	78	8 396	76
Wages	4 000	36	4 100	39
Net margin	4 600	42	4 296	37
Other costs	1 750	16	1 800	16
Net profit	£2 850	26	£2 496	21

* Rooms would be deleted in the case of popular restaurants.
† Percentage of food sales.

Chain operations will collate the same information on weekly or monthly returns and the accounts records will be produced centrally, probably by mechanical or electronic means. Subsidiary controls will be simple food control systems, such as statistical food control described in Chapter 17 based on a food goods inwards book.

Medium-class restaurants (B and C markets)

This group will include licensed restaurants such as steak houses and restaurants of medium-sized hotels (up to 50 rooms). In some cases, restaurants of this size and grade will enjoy an extremely high volume of sales and will use more sophisticated controls than are shown here. However, these are comparatively few and it is for the individual caterer to decide whether more complex systems will justify the savings made.

It is at this size of operation that the 'long form' of accounts will be justified showing wages and costs analysed by department. Each department, rooms, food and liquor, will be further analysed upon schedules to the accounts. Examples of these schedules are shown in *Figures 20.2–20.13*. Obviously, restaurants will not complete the accommodation (rooms) schedule or the accommodation section in the front sheet.

By utilising departmental accounts the caterer has provided himself with a simple form of manpower control upon a budgetary control basis described in the previous chapter.

SUPPLEMENTARY CONTROLS

The control of food in the operation will still not require any more sophisticated method than statistical control and the liquor control system described on p. 221. Restaurants and operations of this size will probably produce a weekly sales report and wages report.

Motorway catering

This type of catering has brought a new phenomenon to the catering industry of the UK in that the operations provide an extremely high volume of sales of cheap, popular foods. Motorway services provide other items such as petrol, oil, breakdown services, and shops, but only the catering aspect is discussed here. The high volume of food sales at low margins demands that accurate and effective food control should be utilised in the organisation. For this purpose standard food cost control is recommended so that all incoming raw materials may be traced through the operation from purchases to service and cash receival.

The comparatively narrow range of dishes served by the operation results in a fairly simple application of the system using not more than some 60 different cost cards.

Motorway service area management also requires adequate monthly management information, preferably showing the various restaurants separately for comparison so that departures from target cost and profit levels will not be hidden. This information is as shown in *Figure 20.15*, page 247.

Department	C	Sales, £	Cost of sales, £	%	Gross margin, £	%	Payroll cost, £	%	Net margin, £	%	Distributed costs, £	%	Profit or loss, £	%
Accommodation	01													
Food	02													
Beverages	03													
Other income	09													
Total operated depts.														
Administration	11													
Sales adverts., etc.	12													
H.L.P.	13													
General	19													
Total														
Control level														
R. & M.	21													
Plant & machinery	22													
Property	23													
Total														
Net profit														

Figure 20.2. Profit and loss report

An operation as large as a motorport will require other reports so that management can continuously monitor every facet of the

Accommodation schedule	£	%
001 Room sales		
051 Public room rent		
Total accommodation sales		
Less:		
091 Allowances to guests		
092 Agency commission		
129 Boarding-out costs		
Net accommodation sales		
131 Gross payroll		
134 Holiday pay		
135 Staff food and beverages		
136 Staff accommodation		
Total payroll cost		
Net margin		
201 Cleaning supplies		
202 Flowers and décor		
203 Magazines and periodicals		
211 Printing and stationery		
271 Laundry and dry cleaning		
272 Cleaning contract		
411 Linen		
412 Uniforms		
Total distributed cost		
Departmental profit		

Figure 20.3. Accommodation schedule

organisation. These will include a daily sales report, a daily cash report and a wages report.

Haute cuisine restaurant

Haute cuisine restaurants serve exotic, carefully prepared (often lovingly prepared) food which more often than not is guided by

Food schedule	£	%
011 Restaurant sales		
031 Banquets		
Coffee shop		
Room service		
Total sales		
Less:		
091 Allowances to guests		
Net sales		
101 Food purchases		
109 Food stock Inc/Dec		
125 Stock losses		
126 Sale of waste (Cr.)		
127 Staff meals (Cr.)		
128 Entertaining (Cr.)		
Total cost of sales		
Gross margin		
131 Gross payroll		
134 Holiday pay		
135 Staff meals and beverages		
136 Staff accommodation		
Total payroll		
Net margin		
201 Catering supplies		
202 Flowers and décor		
211 Printing and stationery		
232 Kitchen fuel		
271 Laundry and dry cleaning		
272 Cleaning contracts		
282 Music and entertainment		
324 Trade licences		
411 Linen		
412 Uniforms		
413 Plate and cutlery		
414 Glass and china		
415 Utensils		
Total distributed costs		
Departmental profit		

Figure 20.4. Food schedule

Beverages and tobacco schedule		£	%
011	Restaurant sales		
021	Bar sales		
031	Banquets		
	Total beverage sales		
091	Allowances to guests		
	Net beverage sales		
111	Beverage purchases		
119	Beverage stock Inc/Dec		
125	Stock losses		
127	Cost of staff drink (Cr.)		
128	Cost of entertainment (Cr.)		
	Cost of beverage sales		
	Gross margin		
131	Gross payroll		
134	Holiday pay		
135	Staff food and drink		
136	Staff accommodation		
	Total payroll		
	Net margin		
201	Beverage department supplies		
202	Flowers and décor		
211	Printing and stationery		
271	Laundry and dry cleaning		
272	Cleaning contracts		
324	Trade licences		
411	Linen		
412	Uniforms		
413	Plate and cutlery		
414	Glass and china		
415	Utensils		
	Total distributed costs		
	Departmental profit		

Figure 20.5. Beverages and tobacco schedule

enthusiasm rather than the menu cost. This is not a bad thing by any means, as is evidenced by the most outstanding of these restaurants.

However, the best restaurants are still businesses and require control. The standard and complexity of food produced by haute

	Other income schedule	£	%
068	Sporting amenities Telephone income Miscellaneous income		
	Total income		
179	Costs of total income		
	Gross margin		
131	Gross payroll		
134	Holiday pay		
135	Staff food and beverages		
136	Staff accommodation		
	Total payroll cost		
	Net margin		
081	Rents received		
082	Commissions and concessions		
083	Profit on exchange		
089	Miscellaneous receipts		
	Total sundry receipts		
	Miscellaneous costs		
	Total other income		

Figure 20.6. Other income schedule

cuisine restaurants frequently cause management problems as the wastage and food losses are difficult to isolate. The only control system which will adequately supply management with information on which they are able to make decisions is standard food cost control.

Fortunately, the fashion amongst restaurateurs is to provide small à la carte menus containing some 30 dishes which are changed every month to three months. This method of operating makes it easy to install standard food costing even if the restaurant is a small one.

Monthly accounts will be produced on the same basis as on page 235. Should the operation be a large one then the long form of accounts may be used (pages 237–246). Liquor control will

Administration schedule		£	%
131	Gross payroll		
134	Holiday pay		
135	Staff food and drink		
136	Staff accommodation		
141	Directors' emoluments		
	Total payroll cost		
203	Subscriptions and donations		
211	Printing and stationery		
261	Telephone and telegrams		
262	Postage		
283	Fees and services		
284	Auditors' remuneration		
321	General insurance		
331	Trade subscriptions		
341	Travel		
342	Entertaining		
391	Cash differences		
392	Cash discounts (Cr.)		
393	Bad debts		
401	Rent of telephones		
402	Internal communications		
412	Uniforms		
	Total distributed cost		
	Departmental cost		

Figure 20.7. Administration schedule

be based upon the par stock control system discussed in Chapter 18 which provides full control of all items purchased, stored and served. Daily and weekly sales reports will be necessary, showing in addition to sales figures important statistics such as average check and diner figures.

Hotel restaurant

The hotel restaurant will obviously be accounted for within the total hotel accounting system which, if a departmental management accounting presentation is used, will include a detailed analysis of restaurant and kitchen operations. An example of this is shown on page 239.

Sales, advertising and promotions schedule	£	%
283 Fees and services		
301 Press advertising		
302 Television and cinema adverts		
303 Direct mail adverts		
304 Brochures and circulars		
305 Posters and placards		
306 Trade gifts		
341 Travel expenses		
342 Entertaining expenses		
412 Uniforms		
Total departmental cost		

Figure 20.8. Sales, advertising and promotions schedule

As yet, very few hotels have adopted any effective system of food control and, therefore, most hoteliers have the choice of a number of systems. For hotel restaurants standard costing is advocated, normally because the presentation of table d'hôte menus necessitates the isolation of a menu composition variance and standard costing is the only system which can provide this.

Heat, light and power schedule	£	%
231 Petrol and oil		
233 Heating fuel		
234 Electric lamps		
251 Electricity		
252 Gas		
253 Water rates		
412 Uniforms		
Departmental cost		

Figure 20.9. Heat, light and power schedule

High-volume restaurants

Very large food operations require a considerable effort in providing control systems. Inevitably, operations of this size cannot rely on the manual production of control information. Caterers for some extraordinary reason seem to resent accounting machinery other than

General schedule		£	%
131	Gross payroll		
134	Holiday pay		
135	Staff food and drink		
136	Staff accommodation		
145	Pension fund		
146	Staff insurance		
147	Training levy		
148	Redundancy pay		
149	Staff transport		
151	Staff recruitment		
152	Staff lodging-out costs		
	Total payroll cost		
231	Motor expenses		
281	Salvage and waste disposal		
411	Uniforms		
	Distributed costs less Staff accommodation (Cr.)		
	Total distributed costs		
	Departmental cost		

Figure 20.10. General schedule

those which record sales. There is no doubt, however, that machinery is both useful and necessary to record costs and present cost information in a meaningful manner. Large restaurants will adopt the same presentation of accounts as those advocated for motorways (see *Figure 20.15*, page 247).

The design of the document will be slightly different to accommodate liquor. This is indicated in *Figure 20.14*, page 246. Supplementary controls will include most or all the examples discussed in the previous chapters on control.

Repairs and maintenance schedule		£	%
131	Gross payroll		
134	Holiday pay		
135	Staff food and drink		
136	Staff accommodation		
	Total payroll cost		
231	Petrol and oil		
241	Materials		
242	Garden supplies		
273	Maintenance costs		
274	Repair charges		
283	Fees and services		
412	Uniforms		
416	Tools		
	Total distributed costs		
	Departmental cost		

Figure 20.11. Repairs and maintenance schedule

Multi-restaurant complex and chain operations

The multi-outlet operation or chain, whether using one common production kitchen or individual kitchens, creates tremendous control problems, as a large number of accounting routines must be considered, possibly involving many different environments.

Plant and machinery schedule		£	%
431	Rent of machinery		
441	Renewal of machinery		
451	Dep. of machinery		
433	Rent of F.F.F.		
443	Renewal F.F.F.		
453	Dep. F.F.F.		
434	Rent of motor vehicle		
454	Dep. of motor vehicle		
	Cost of plant and machinery		

Figure 20.12. Plant and machinery schedule

Property schedule		£	%
461	Rates		
462	Insurance		
471	Ground rent		
472	Rental		
485	Amortisation—long term leases		
486	Amortisation—short term leases		
	Total property		

Figure 20.13. Property schedule

This renders decision-taking and action a complex problem. The major step is to obtain information extremely rapidly so that time is gained to make rational and subsequently effective decisions.

Very rarely do manual systems provide an effective answer to the situation. Therefore, the answer appears to lie in the use of accounting equipment with short lines of communication for input and output information. A considerable range of equipment is available from simple single-register mechanical accounting machines, costing from £200, to teletyper input to a computer configuration, either through buying time or by an installation at head office.

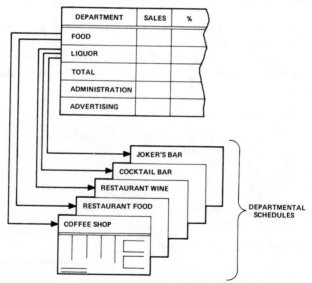

Figure 20.14. High-volume restaurant accounts system

Department	Sales, £	Cost of sales, £	%	Gross margin, £	%	Wages, £	%	Net margin, £	%	Distribution costs, £	%	Net profit, £	%
The Golden Fillet	100 000	35 000	35	65 000	65	30 000	30	35 000	35	5 000	5	30 000	30
Cafeteria	150 000	60 000	40	90 000	60	32 000	21	58 000	39	6 000	4	52 000	35
Workman's Café	160 000	72 000	45	88 000	55	32 000	20	56 000	35	4 800	3	51 200	32
Total operated departments	410 000	167 000	41	243 000	59	94 000	23	149 000	36	15 800	4	133 200	32
Administration						7 000				2 400		9 400	2
Advertising										4 000		4 000	1
Heat, light, power										10 000		10 000	2
General										4 000		4 000	1
Total	—	—		—		£7 000		—		£20 400		£27 400	6
Control level	410 000	167 000	41	243 000	59	101 000	25	142 000	34	36 200	8	105 800	26
Rent, rates, insur.										87 000		87 000	22
Repairs & maintenance						3 500				17 800		21 300	5
Depreciation										10 000		10 000	2
Total						3 500				114 800		118 300	29
Net profit	—	£167 000	41	£243 000	59	£104 500	26	£138 500	34	£151 000	37	(£12 500)	(3)

Figure 20.15. Profit and loss report for motorway catering

This is not to say that sophisticated equipment answers all problems. But carefully purchased or hired equipment producing meaningful management information is available and necessary to the success of any large operation. The role of computers in catering is discussed in Chapter 22 in some detail.

DECISION-TAKING BASED ON CONTROL INFORMATION

Control systems cost money to operate and there is no point in installing sophisticated systems if management are unable to make decisions and take action on the basis of the information provided by the systems. This section of the chapter deals with the final information provided by control systems and the method of decision-taking and action derived from it.

Food control results

The food control systems advocated in this book all produce results analysed over food sub-headings. The two simpler controls, namely statistical and direct cost systems, produce total variances from expected cost, as shown in *Table 20.4.* Items that appear out of line in relation to total consumption and mix of consumption would be subjected to the following examination:

(a) A check on goods inwards and storage routines.
(b) A check on prices paid that week for individual items.
(c) An examination of the use of particular items in relevant section of the kitchen.
(d) A careful consideration of what has changed from the week before, e.g.:
  (i)   Supplier, price and quality.
  (ii) Goods inwards.
  (iii) Preparation.
  (iv) Service.
  (v)   Staff.
  (vi) Measurement of (a) against (b) and (c).
  (vii) Isolation of the reason for difference.
  (viii) Consideration of action to satisfactorily eliminate deviation.
  (ix) Taking of action.
  (x)   A follow-up in subsequent weeks.

Table 20.4 Food control variances

Meat 1	Fish 2	Poultry 3	Fruit, veg. 4	Groceries 5	Bread, cake 6	Tea, coffee 7	Milk, cream 8	Sundries 9
£96	£44	£18	£10	£14	£7	£5	£4	£1

The fact that the variances are broken down over a number of heads allows differences in performance to be analysed quickly, decisions made and action taken. A more effective method of control of food is standard food costing which will give the variances shown in *Figure 20.16*. The standard food costing variances schedule shows a full breakdown of variances which would be dealt with in the following manner.

INFORMATION

The high *meat* stock held the previous week has been run down to an acceptable level. *Grocery* stocks, although extremely high, have not been run down to a low enough level, and a further reduction of £100 stock is necessary. *Tea and coffee* stocks are too high and should be reduced to £20–£30 during the next week.

DECISION

To put dry stores stocks on to a mini-max stock system and spot check all other stores items.

ACTION

To arrange that management are notified of items exceeding maximum so that instructions to reduce may be made.

INFORMATION

Staff feeding costs are too low and are masking the gross profit made by the food operation. Total variance excluding staff feeding credit variance is 6%. The shortage of staff feeding expenditure is £100 for the week.

DECISION

To instruct the chef to adhere to the correct portions and menu specifications for staff food.

ACTION

The instruction is to be followed by spot checks on staff feeding throughout the next week.

Item	Code	Opening stock, £	Purchases @ standard, £	Closing stock, £	Consumption @ standard, £	Staff feeding, £	Cost of sales, £	Meals served	Usage variances, £	Price variances, £	Total variances £
Meat	1	350	1 000	120	1 230	60	1 170	1 070	100	69	169
Fish	2	110	650	80	680	20	660	550	110	73	183
Poultry	3	50	420	60	410	15	395	365	30	20	50
Fruit, veg.	4	105	480	70	515	23	492	442	50	15	65
Groceries	5	420	600	350	670	30	640	590	50	15	65
Tea, coffee	6	80	150	80	150	10	140	135	5	8	13
Bread, cake	7	20	150	15	155	12	143	140	3	—	3
Milk, cream	8	35	180	25	190	30	160	158	2	—	2
Sundries	9										
Total		£1 170	£3 630	£800	£4 000	£200	£3 800	3 450	£350	£200	£550

* Staff feeding variance
difference between actual
consumption and :
Allowance × No. staff × 7 days
= Correct margin

	£	%
Total sales	10 000	100
Actual gross profit	6 000	60
Standard gross profit	6 500	65
Total variance	£500	5

	£	%
Usage variance	350	3·5
Price variance	200	2·0
*Staff feeding variance	(100)	(1·0)
Menu composition variance	50	5
Total variance	£500	5

Figure 20.16. Standard food cost variances schedule

INFORMATION

Usage variances total £350 or 10% of meal cost at standard, which is unacceptable. The main wastage constituents are meat, fish, poultry, fruit and veg. and groceries.

DECISION

To interview chef and kitchen staff regarding past weeks' menus to isolate change in portions. This may have been due to inferior low yield goods or lack of security.

ACTION

Change buying specification plus personal checks on incoming goods or tighten kitchen security to achieve correct portion control.

INFORMATION

Price variances total £200, mainly composed of meat, fish and poultry prices. Previous weeks' invoices would be examined to isolate high prices, and the reasons obtained for same.

DECISION

To change suppliers or buy alternative items to decrease price or alter menu composition.

ACTION

To adopt one of the courses above.

INFORMATION

Menu composition variance totals £50, indicating that menu dish costs are out of line. Examination of past weeks' menus will take place to find which did not yield the required gross margin by virtue of dishes purchased.

DECISION

To ensure that similar dish combinations do not recur.

LIQUOR CONTROL

The information provided by the par stock liquor control system is as follows:

(a) Excess stocks in cellars and bars.

(b) Purchasing signals for cellar re-stocking.

(c) Cellar stock losses.

(d) Foreign liquor in bars.

(e) Bar gross profits and surplus/deficit.

The decisions and action taken by caterers from the above information is fairly straightforward.

Management accounts

The information provided by management accounts indicates the total economic position of an operating unit in broad terms so that management may assess the total activities of the organisation. The best way to isolate deviations from acceptable economic performance is by utilising the simple technique of budgetary control in conjunction with management accounts. Many textbooks, for example, Fearn, D.A., *Management Systems for the Hotel, Catering and Allied Industries*, Business Books, London (1969), discuss budgetary control and, therefore, it is not proposed to describe the technique in detail. As an example, consider the hotel front sheet shown in *Figure 20.17*. This shows a number of variances from budget. These variances are not readily identifiable from this document, and recourse will be made to individual costs on departmental schedules which will indicate which particular costs are out of line.

Therefore, the following further information will also be isolated (*Table 20.5*). This information will provide management with data for decision-taking through the assessment of the differences between present circumstances and those existent when the budget was constructed. Action will be taken to eliminate the differences from budget.

SUMMARY

The decision-making, action-taking sequence

GATHER INFORMATION

Do not take decisions based upon inadequate information.

Item	Actual this period		Budget this period		Variance this period		
	£	%	£	%	£	+/−	
Sales							
Accommodation	10 000	100	10 000	100			
Food	8 000	100	8 000	100			
Liquor	5 000	100	5 000	100			
Total	£23 000	100	£23 000	100			
Cost of sales							
Food	3 360	42	2 800	35	560	−7	→Action
Liquor	2 750	55	2 500	50	250	−5	→Action
Total	£6 110	29	£5 300	23	£810	−6	
Gross margin	16 890	71	17 700	77	810	−6	
Wages and staff costs	7 130	31	6 900	30	230	−1	→Action
Net margin	9 760	40	10 800	47	1 040	−7	
Administration	460	2	690	3	(230)	+1	→Action
Advertising	690	3	460	2	230	−1	→Action
Heat, light, power	920	4	690	3	230	−1	→Action
General expenses	920	4	920	4	—		
Total controllable costs	£2 990	13	£2 760	12	£230	−1	
Hotel control level	6 770	27	8 040	35	1 270	−8	
Rent, rates, ins.	240	1	240	1	—		
Other additions	120	—	120	—	—		
Depreciation	460	2	460	2	—		
Reps. and mainten.	350	1	350	1	—		
Total non-controllable costs	£1 170	5	£1 170	5	—		
Net profit	£5 600	22	£6 870	30	£1 270	−8	

Figure 20.17. Specimen hotel front sheet

Table 20.5 Additional variances

Item	£±	Source
Food cost	560−	From food control system
Liquor cost	250−	From liquor control system
Wages costs	230−	From wages schedule and manpower control
Administration	230+	From administration schedule
Advertising	230−	From advertising schedule
Heat, light, power	230−	From heat, light, power schedule
Total variances	£1 270	

ISOLATE DIFFERENCES IN CIRCUMSTANCES

Staff, methods, policy and materials usage.

IDENTIFY DIFFERENCE CAUSING DEVIATION

Eliminate alternatives.

ELIMINATE DIFFERENCE

FOLLOW THROUGH TO MAINTAIN ELIMINATION

21
Training

STAFF TRAINING

The absence of trained staff in the catering industry is a problem which has many important side-effects. This is true of other industries also, e.g. tourism where lack of trained personnel poses a serious threat to continuous growth in tourism.

In catering, however, the main objections to training are that:

(a) Staff have to be off duty for training sessions.

(b) It costs money.

(c) Staff may leave, thereby allowing another operator to benefit from any training.

These views are, of course, short-sighted in the extreme, as well-trained and certificated staff amply repay the expenditure and lost duty hours necessitated by training sessions. Further, young people are not interested in entering an industry where training is merely a question of watching someone else. Consequently, little professional respect is given to hotel and catering employees by the world at large.

One could further outline the consequences of the lack of training facilities and environment in the catering industry. But the majority of caterers are now only too well aware of these. Unfortunately, as training on a wide scale is comparatively new to the industry, great confusion exists as to its objectives and purposes—much of it having no impact whatsoever. These objectives and purposes are summarised in *Table 21.1.*

Craft skills

The industry has been very conscious of craft skills as opposed to management skills. But the emphasis is now being concentrated on acquisition of management skills with which to temper craft. This is, of course, not to say that craft is unimportant—it is, but only if the skills gained are to be used. It seems wasteful to instruct students in subjects which they will never use, because it lengthens training

Table 21.1 Objectives and purposes of training

Objective	Purpose
A full grasp of the craft skills necessary to discharge the job adequately	To ensure that the job required to be done by the 'living establishment' is done in accordance with the particular meal experience aimed at
Ability to communicate with the customer	To understand fully and appreciate the customer's needs. To recognise and rapidly eliminate problematic situations
Understanding of the job situation in relation to the organisation	To be able to recognise side-effects of actions and situations. To encourage inter-departmental co-operation
Preparation for a superior or alternative position	To absorb the skills necessary to discharge new duties competently
Ability to teach the job to someone else	To ensure staff over which one has authority are taught adequately and correctly

and may invite an overall shallow competence rather than considerable skill and dexterity focused upon a narrow range of entirely necessary duties. Staff, therefore, should only be trained in those jobs which are entirely necessary to their success in the specific positions which they hold. For example, an extensive course in waiting is not necessary for someone who serves plated meals.

The Brick System of training, introduced by the HCITB for various types of work including waiting and beverage service, is designed on those lines. Only those jobs which require to be done will be incorporated into the training programme.

On the subject of craft training one often comes across the controversy of management trainees working through departments and those who are college trained. Some colleges offer sandwich courses, the students being obliged to work in specific departments during the summer vacation—others do not. Requirements also differ for varying students. Owner-managers of small operations would require a craft bias because they must be available to fill in where needed. Managers working in large operations must be more aware of managerial skills—there is, therefore, no one acceptable formula of management training. A reasonable provision for both requirements must be provided either by specialist schools or by specialist courses.

A great deal of work is being done in this area although the differences between courses and colleges are not always apparent to the would-be student.

Communication with customers

The social skills of staff in their dealings with customers is an important yet seldom considered field of training. It is normally left to an individual's disposition as to his attitude in dealing with the customer. However, it is essential that staff give a good impression to the customer, because this is part of what he is paying for.

An analysis of social requirements is as follows:

(a) Cheerfulness.
(b) Awareness (observations of the customer's needs without being asked).
(c) Politeness.
(d) Articulation.
(e) Good grooming.
(f) Helpfulness.
(g) Respect.

The only way that these skills may be imparted is by constant *tactful* guidance by management in conjunction with case study sessions indicating the various problems. Courses set up by people capable of gaining confidence and putting the subject across as well as guiding case studies have been found very helpful by many companies.

Understanding of the job situation in relation to the organisation

The employee who understands the effect of his actions upon other departments and the organisation as a whole will be able to work more effectively than if he is totally unaware of other departmental responsibilities, and the cost and profit structure of the firm. It seems to be a common fallacy amongst certain caterers that the people they employ are unable either to appreciate or understand the way the establishment works or the importance of controlling costs. In fact, experience indicates that the opposite would tend to be true. Staff appreciate being told what is going on and feel a sense of participation and belonging as a result.

The strategy may be connected with a bonus scheme based upon excess of actual profits over budget. This particular scheme is one which has worked extremely well in a number of diverse organisations. In order for it to work, however, staff must be taught how the organisation works and the relevance of cost and profit levels. A bonus to the organisation is normally the build-up of enthusiasm and the suggestions and voluntary work that ensues from a deliberate show of confidence such as this.

Preparation for a superior or alternative position

When staff are promoted to a superior position or to another department, invariably they are thrown into the middle of the job without any training or instruction. Consequently, there is a considerable time lag whilst the new man is learning by 'feel' and is obviously not working most effectively.

As with most learning problems, new appointees tend to experience difficulties in adjusting to the concept of total responsibility, whereas they find the details easy to assimilate. An example of this is the hotel assistant manager who is promoted to manager. From being responsible for certain isolated duties the assistant becomes responsible for a total business organisation with which he inevitably takes some time to become conversant.

A structure of courses should be available so that staff appointed to new positions are able to appreciate the total concept, authority and responsibility of the job. This course structure has worked very well for newly appointed foremen and line managers, also for salesmen and sales managers. So far a similar scheme has not been evolved for the hotel and catering industry, although some course programmes are tending to be structured in this way.

Ability to teach the job to somebody else

The HCITB have operated their on-the-job and instructor training courses for some time with a certain measure of success. The courses illustrate to departmental heads the need to train in daily work and the right way to go about it. One cannot hope to promote personnel easily or even allow them to work unsupervised without some degree of training. Therefore, it is desirable that the operation's hierarchy allows a continued on-the-job training effort right down the line.

A famous American industrialist revolutionised training and the organisation by stipulating that:

(a) Every member of staff should be training somebody for his job.

(b) Every member of staff should be being trained for the next job.

If training of this nature is not carried out upon an overall and disciplined basis it tends to be a waste of time. It must work hand in hand with a logical promotional progression because once it is seen not to work staff will become apathetic and disinterested. Obviously, there is not room for every member of the catering staff to progress. However, it should be realised that each member of staff will work more happily and, therefore, be more efficient if he knows that the interest shown in his work and development will stand him in good stead in the future. Even if that future is with another organisation.

SUMMARY

Staff training falls into a number of defined areas:

(a) *Basic job skills.* College or on-the-job training.

(b) *Social skills.* Internal courses and day-to-day management guidance.

(c) *Job situation and the organisation.* Induction courses, preferably operated by outside organisations although large companies may find that they are able to run them on an internal basis.

(d) *Preparation for a superior or alternative position.*

(e) *Ability to teach the job to somebody else.* HCITB, on-the-job training or instructor training courses.

The training programme above covers the basic objectives of staff at work. However, many organisations consider other aspects of training to be important. Whilst no objection is raised to alternative training concepts, it is essential that the above basic requirements are thoroughly satisfied before embarking upon further training.

MANAGEMENT TRAINING

The subject of management training is a very controversial issue in the industry at the moment because so many different views are taken of what a manager's responsibilities actually are. They might range from being totally responsible for everything in an organisation, to varying degrees of limitation, to no responsibility whatsoever. Without discussing the responsibilities that managers ought to have, one must consider whether the term 'management' is an applicable one. Most of the industry's training problems in the management field arise because of the diverse interpretation of the management function.

Management

A manager takes decisions upon the basis of data received, and delegates the action culminating from that decision to other people in order to achieve a defined objective. He is, therefore, akin to a military commander who is given objectives and must devise strategy (short-term plans) to achieve these objectives by utilising his resources (men, materials, plant and buildings) to the best advantage.

From the above, it may be readily realised that many managers are, in fact, supervisors and very occasionally vice versa. Whatever the local situation may be it is important to rationalise the functions in terms of training needs. This means that training officers and others who are responsible for selecting courses should consider very carefully the role that their own management undertake, and the level at which the courses are set. It is of little benefit, for example, in spending £200 on a course in decision-making and action if the manager is never permitted to make a major decision.

At the current time there are many courses open to management, most of which have been stimulated by the fact that fees may be refunded by the HCITB to companies participating. Because of this it is difficult for organisations to select a training programme from the many alternatives which are available.

The increase of management knowledge must be considered in direct relation to the company's management and growth objectives. Most courses are concerned with one of three areas:

(a) Techniques.

(b) A field of study, e.g. sales, marketing, accounting.

(c) Approaches to management problems, e.g. decision-making, communications, etc.

This is the first assessment one should make of available courses. The next is to grade each area in terms of one's own personnel. The third is to consider which of the courses would benefit the company in real terms, either in the near or distant future. For example, in terms of techniques, there is little point in management being instructed in the niceties of computer technology if the company is not likely to own a computer or, even if it has one, is not likely to have much to do with it. Certain techniques are, of course, very useful to management, such as critical path analysis, discounted cash flow, and work study methods.

General management courses are the most useful base as it is these courses which convey to managers the broad field of management, and from which they are able to select subjects for further study which they believe to be most relevant to their needs. Considerable opportunities of development are open to management and it is not always easy to select the right course of instruction. Consequently, management courses do not always enjoy popularity. For this reason it is essential that a correct selection is made.

22
Future of food and beverage operations

The future operating methods of food and beverage operations are merely being hinted at today. However, those trends which make economic and marketing sense will become accepted by the industry in general once prejudice and traditional opposition have died in the face of declining profits. Some of these, which may occur in the course of the next decade, are outlined below.

MANAGEMENT PRINCIPLES AND PRACTICE

The sudden interest stimulated in management development by the HCITB grants, declining profits, and increased taxation, was really felt by the industry from 1967 to 1970. Much of the credit for this is due to two leading catering consultancy firms who invested considerable sums in extensive management development programmes. As is common to most interests stimulated on an industry-wide front, thoughts and progress have been spasmodic and muddled, to say the least.

Analysis would show five basic approaches to management development in the industry at present.

Technique training

This approach is one which was adopted by the HCITB initially and by several other organisations. The disadvantage is that management learn a great many of the techniques which without the background of management principles do not become used or useful because management forget them, do not become fully conversant with their application, or do not understand that techniques are management tools which are merely aids to management and are not substitutes for management itself. It is hoped, some authorities would believe inevitable, that technique training will cease in the early seventies in favour of total management development. The reason for the situation as it is at present is characteristic of the other methods of management development discussed in this chapter. In other words, not enough people in the industry really understand the nature of management and, therefore, adopt techniques which are easy to learn and to teach.

Basic skills

Some companies are convinced that their managers know how to manage and are adopting the approach of teaching them techniques supposedly useful to their day-to-day work. Such techniques include speed reading, letter-writing courses, salesmanship and public speaking. There are two reasons for this approach. One is that management philosophy and the way the company does things are at variance and there is little point in teaching things which the company will never adopt. The second is that many companies send management on many doubtful courses in order to obtain cash refunds from the HCITB; the value of courses is secondary to the fact that the cash is to be refunded through the grant system.

Financial bias

There is a basic confusion in the industry aggravated by the trade press and consultancy firms, who should know better, that management is financial control and marketing is selling. This is an unfortunate legacy from the USA where financial control and salesmanship are very pronounced sectors of catering operations, and are the two which impress themselves most on managers who visit that country, to the exclusion of all else. This interpretation of the management function is one which will be surpassed by a more rational approach when the trade press, management books and consultants speak with one voice on management matters.

Sensitivity training

Some very large companies have come to the conclusion that a basic management problem is communication and have, therefore, utilised various management training techniques based upon sensitivity training ideas. The question of sensitivity training is one which is controversial in management matters at the moment and is likely to be so for some years to come. Consideration and study of a wide variety of behavioural techniques, including 'T' groups, management grid, etc., have cast some doubt on their usefulness for the following reasons:

(a) Any training programme which may invade an individual's privacy or endanger his health, mental or physical, should not be tolerated.

(b) Companies who hope to improve communications may find greater improvement by changing procedures rather than behaviour.

(c) The techniques are basically destructive and teach (perhaps inadvertently) destructive analysis, a change in behaviour apparent in most people who have undergone sensitivity training. Destructive analysis has no virtue because the act of tearing an idea, method, or object to shreds bypasses any *constructive* idea which may be gained from it.

Management function in relation to market selection and exploitation

One approach to management is the consideration of the objectives of the management function in direct relation to the business functions of market selection and exploitation, together with operating at least average cost.

This is the approach which recommends itself, as it has been shown to work,* which is more than may be said of the training concepts described above. One of the main objectives of business is to make money by adequately satisfying a market. Logically, the best development a manager may have, therefore, is to learn the basic principles of the system of management, whose main objects are as follows:

(a) Satisfaction of market needs.

(b) Maintenance of growth of assets.

(c) Achievement of acceptable return on capital.

Misunderstandings of the meaning of management lead to irrelevant and wasteful training procedures, or the adoption of sophisticated procedures by firms who have not ensured that their managers

---

* FEARN, D. A., *Management Systems for the Hotel, Catering and Allied Industries*, Business Books, London (1969).

are fully conversant with the principles of management philosophy. Management is the achievement of defined long- and short-term objectives through other people. It is difficult to understand how many management concepts contribute to this—and any concept which does not contribute to the achievement of management objectives becomes a luxury.

Most management development authorities accept that it is essential for managers to fully understand the nature of management before embarking on the acquisition of management techniques. Techniques are aids to management not a substitute for it. Management is a continuous process which utilises certain tools from time to time to carry out a particular task more efficiently; a carpenter carries out his trade continuously although he would only use certain tools, e.g. a spokeshave, for a particular job.

Having discussed the importance of management principles in management development one must consider how to train management to use them—the greatest criticism of management training (and rightly so) is that it seldom adds to the well-being of the company in terms of profit or otherwise. This is normally because whilst managers are taught the right way to manage they are rarely taught how to go about it. Allied, therefore, to a thorough understanding of the principles of management there must be an adoption of a systematic approach which would encompass communications, problem-solving, decision-making, building on strength, teamwork and the many other skills necessary to the dynamic line manager. A very constructive approach is advocated by 'training partnerships', known as Coverdale Training, which is recommended to anyone who is interested in the above.

A full understanding of the nature of management is not an easy thing to obtain. However, one would postulate that it is highly necessary to the continued optimum success of any business enterprise. This is becoming rapidly apparent to students of management who have studied the leisure industries, and will become common knowledge during the next decade.

CENTRALISATION

The effects, advantages and disadvantages of commissary operations which are creating considerable interest in the USA and UK have already been discussed in Chapter 9. This is but one indication of organisations taking advantage of economies of scale. There are obvious indications of the trend, e.g. co-operative marketing groups such as *Prestige* and *Interchange*, as well as group buying schemes, labour pools, and inter-hotel comparison to name but a few areas. So far, where effort and resources have been centralised (except for commonly owned units) this has been on a fairly informal basis. However, it is expected that the co-operation will become more formal to the extent of the formation of hotel and restaurant chains and true co-operative societies.

The amount of effort required for one unit's marketing/accounting/purchasing programme, etc., is not much less than for two or three units and remains inverse up to twelve or more. It is, therefore, sound economics to centralise such services and minimise the cost to each participating unit. The artificial business incentives of the sixties (the will to survive) have resulted in a considerably more progressive attitude to economies of this kind than hitherto. In fact, the attitude change has really taken place since 1967–8 and should the momentum become more rapid there is no doubt that the evolution outlined above is likely to be here before 1975.

MARKETING

It is clear that the large and medium-sized companies are taking a greater interest in marketing and that UK hoteliers and caterers are leading world leisure in this field. In this context, marketing is not to be confused with selling—they are two quite different, although inter-related, functions. Marketing is the design of a product for a specified market; selling is telling that market about it. The hardsell US approach is not marketing and it is unfortunate that this confusion is still apparent even in large companies.

It can be seen that more caterers are considering their market in terms of total product design than before. One reason for this is that competition obliges them to be able to satisfy the market better than their opposition, hence the desire to satisfy market need better than it does. This interest has given rise to market research techniques to determine market needs by many companies and institutions. As yet, most of their techniques are unsophisticated. However, it is certain that the interest shown will stimulate the discovery of more sophisticated tools within the next few years.

DIVERSIFICATION

Many industries are on the fringe of leisure. Therefore, it is not surprising that some large companies have considered leisure in their diversification programmes. The results of this will be to increase leisure investment rapidly as most of these companies are very large and the size of the investment, to have any impact, must of necessity be in terms of millions. As even the largest leisure operations, with the exception of one or two, are not in the category of large companies the effect will be to increase national and international investment substantially. Together with this there will be an insistence by these companies of a managerial approach rather than that of the traditional caterer, which will have the effect of stimulating management thinking in the industry.

One can visualise the effect of catering managers working for the first time alongside their industrial counterparts who, in the main, have absorbed a totally different management philosophy. The effects are already beginning to be felt by those companies who are diversifying, in terms of the number of applications for management posts from intelligent young men who realise the development advantages available in such an environment.

The obvious effect of substantial investment will make leisure big business in terms of individual organisations, which will enhance the political and social pressures of the industry as a voice to be heard and as a desirable industry in which to work.

THE FINANCIAL MYTH

The financial myth of accepting accounting as being more than just a stewardship function is likely to be exploded in the foreseeable future. Accounting is not management. It is either one or both of the following:

(a) Figures produced at year end on which tax computation is based. Normally they are produced much too late for any management purpose and are generally far from meaningful.

(b) Figures produced for management information to inform management of their performance in relation to budgets.

In some cases (a) and (b) are the same figures prepared to illustrate an accurate financial position, and presented in such a way that management easily understands them.

Because systems have been evolved and heavily publicised which can satisfy both requirements, management in the industry have tended to place more importance on these than is necessary. The unfortunate by-product of this view is that other sectors of the management system have enjoyed very little interest and publicity, e.g. personnel relations–administration, sales, marketing, training, etc.

It is absolutely essential to operate an effective accounting system and to produce meaningful control data, but management reports must be relegated to their correct place in the management system. Accounting and control information is merely a system of signals which indicate whether a business, a department within that business, or a cost within that department, is straying from a planned path. The planned path is produced in the form of a budget. Further, the most elaborate system is entirely useless if recipients of reports are confused and overawed by the documentation they receive. The purpose of control data is to provide management with a signal that a decision must be made and action taken. The data will indicate, as far as possible, what direction that decision and action is likely to take. Due to the incredible amount of publicity which accounting has received in the trade press during the last few years, the function of accounting has been exaggerated out of all proportion. Consequently, a large amount of erroneous information has been collected and it is about time that accounting was shown to be the modest stewardship function that it is. There are very few managers who really understand the function of the accounts which they receive from expensively maintained control and accounting departments. Therefore, they prefer to manage by 'feel', rather than use the information with which they are provided.

The above is a situation which cannot exist for very long in a dynamic and knowledgeable industry, and will be obviated by the pressures of management evolution and economic necessity.

To put hotel and catering accounts in perspective, it should be realised that the accounts and controls in use are virtually the simplest available, when one considers the intricacies of batch, marginal, standard and direct costing, and integrated accounts that many industrial managers contend with.

COMPUTER TECHNOLOGY

Computers are helpful machines capable of carrying out millions of calculations in a few seconds. But, as yet, except for the few relatively large companies, equipment of this nature is not generally worth while. However, with the possibility of co-operative use on a bureau basis it is valid to discuss what computers actually do.

Because of the speed of the machine a bureau user would be 'on line', i.e. in connection by teletyper to computer input/output, for a few minutes per day. The diagram (*Figure 22.1*) indicates the way in which the computer could deal with such information. The input would be reservations, ordering, stock control, sleeper/diner trends, food and beverage revenue control, maintenance programmes, guest accounting, etc.

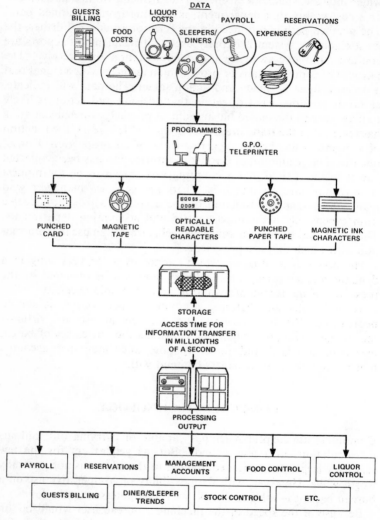

Figure 22.1. The computer — a caterer's eye view

Because of the huge number of constant factors and the relatively few variables involved it becomes a simple matter to provide a programme to deal with the sums. A computer, however, must be told what to do and input of data must therefore, be accurate—but so must it be for manual or other means of computation in order that the built-in checks are not a disadvantage.

Because businesses may be linked with a computer through a teleprinter input/output, a bureau may service a considerable number of operations. Obviously, the use of computing equipment represents a very large step for a co-operative or small chain. However, cheaper and smaller equipment is being produced continuously and a number of such installations will be made by the 1980s.

FOOD AND BEVERAGE TRENDS

Many informed guesses are made as to future trends of food and beverage operations, varying from indications of new food fashions to types of service. To consider properly the future of food and beverage operations in terms of product one must inevitably commence the analysis from two areas:

(a) The needs of the market and changes in the composition of the market.

(b) The availability or otherwise of resources such as raw materials, labour and capital.

Market trends

Observation of the market trends would indicate the following changes:

(a) The gradual unpopularity of haute cuisine restaurants.

(b) Increase in fast service operations.

(c) The provision of a compromise between (a) and (b) culminating in fast food service operation with atmosphere.

(d) The interest of the market in restaurants with atmosphere (mood).

The changes in market composition have taken place at the extremities. This has had the effect of compressing the market income levels, reducing the difference between the rich and not so rich. For example, a few years ago many categories of workers had an average income of £15 per week or lower. The size of this group has diminished and the same trades are enjoying wages of

£20–£40 per week. This general change in economic outlook for millions of people has had its effect on the eating-out situation generally. At the other end of the market, however, the opposite trend seems to be occurring, in that the very rich are diminishing in numbers. They are being replaced by entrepreneurs and captains of industry who, through background and environment, prefer a substantially different atmosphere to the haute cuisine or gourmet restaurant.

In general terms the market has learnt to discriminate and the conventional operation where the only creative job is to cook the food is no longer acceptable. Much of the interest in being invited to a new friend's house is to see the structure, character, if any, and the manner in which it is decorated—it is precisely the same with an eating establishment. People become bored if they know that they are going to receive basically the same food served in the same way in the same environment. The market is demanding a meal experience from the restaurants it patronises; to some caterers this represents the need for a gimmick, to few it means the careful and sensitive provision of mood. This has been discussed earlier in depth in Chapter 3.

Resources

The attraction of labour has become extremely difficult, basically because too many operations are chasing too few staff. It is not a situation which can be remedied overnight. Therefore, caterers must take it into account when planning new operations.

Capital is also scarce or, if available, only at high interest rates. Therefore, fixed and working capital must work hard to justify its existence. This has encouraged the careful use of capital in new operations and has resulted in less waste of space, less over-equipping and stronger interest in financial data and control procedures. There is also a greater interest in location requirements in terms of the market.

The availability of prepared raw materials has encouraged many caterers to buy pre-portioned, partially or wholly pre-cooked meals, prepared vegetables and the like, which tends to violate the most popular items, standardising foodstuffs in a great many operations. Inevitably, the only difference that caterers can provide is in terms of presentation. Many establishments create interesting presentations from standard foodstuffs which have been designed with the mood of the operation in mind. Many others do not, presenting a tired menu and food to go with it.

Summary

(a) Compression of market income variation.

(b) Interest of the market in mood (atmosphere).

(c) Popularity of fast food service operations.

(d) Scarcity of labour.

(e) Scarcity of capital.

(f) Trend to standardise foodstuffs.

Conclusion

The factors above, in isolation, would indicate the elimination of haute cuisine operations. This is, of course, unlikely because any man-produced product retains its hand-made élite and this is equally true of catering. However, the haute cuisine operations which do survive will be extremely few, very expensive and well-operated establishments.

The provision of mood, scarcity of labour and provision of pre-prepared foodstuffs, together with scarcity of capital, will lead to a new type of operation some of which are in existence and proving in practical performance the results of this analysis.

The operations will be carefully located in high population catchment areas where access by the hotel population will be relatively easy. The creation of mood will be fundamental to the success of the operations and, therefore, design and building costs are likely to be higher than formerly considered by restaurateurs. An explanation of this is that restaurants do not normally have a long life and tend to be sold after a short period for very little, the only profit accruing to the operator being in terms of revenue earnings during the restaurant's life.

The alternative is to create something which is so successful at depicting a particular mood that it is timeless. The initial capital cost is high but the restaurant has a far longer life, and because of a consistent turnover over a long period enjoys a capital profit on sale. An example of this is *Sands*, in New Bond Street, which, although several years old, is still one of the most popular restaurants in London, retaining an atmosphere which eludes everyone who tries to copy it.

Because of labour shortage one must obviously utilise what is available to the full, and also reduce the need for skilled staff to a minimum. This can be done in two ways:

(a) By remaining open all day so that the staff are used to generate sales other than luncheon and dinner. To do this a careful design is necessary to encompass the coffee shop and restaurant sections.

(b) By utilising modern cooking (microwave, convector), purchasing (pre-portioned and pre-prepared goods), and service techniques to reduce staff establishment and necessary skills.

The conservation of capital is dealt with in an entirely different way from that generally accepted in the past. It was usual for a restaurateur to spend only the minimum required to operate. Normally, this was because the site was leased and, therefore, belonged to someone else. Consequently, it was not desirable to spend considerable sums on another's property. Other reasons were that it was generally considered that restaurants had short lives and heavy expenditure would not be desirable in the event of a change of design to accommodate a new trend. Also, little thought was given to the mood and totality of the operation in terms of market needs.

The new trend is to ensure that an appropriate mood is achieved which inevitably costs money for design, building and possibly research. The approach is concerned with the overall financial picture which takes into account a substantial return over a period of ten years rather than two or three. Obviously, if one is wrong then the potential losses are greater. However, professional food and beverage management should not be wrong if they have approached the project as skilled managers.

At the lower end of the market, substantial changes have already taken place. As it became obvious that people were rapidly tiring of the cafés and snack bars of the fifties and early sixties, some companies found that they could provide food in an acceptable atmosphere at an economic price. The success of these operations was phenomenal and one company in particular enjoyed one of the fastest growth records of all quoted companies, catering or otherwise. Because of the narrow range of food such operations are able to provide, the market tends to tire of them quickly or visits them at long intervals. The US answer to this problem is one which will probably be adopted in the UK. This is the central commissary operations supplying large chains. An example would be the Marriot Corporation's Hot Shoppes. The advantage of the commissary is that foodstuffs may be purchased more cheaply and are economically produced. Further, research facilities will be available to provide new dishes to give continuous change and variety.

Three major market sectors only have been discussed, although, of course, food operations may be analysed into several different types. It is believed, however, that the major changes are likely to be those outlined above and will affect those three sectors most pertinently.

EQUIPMENT AND PROCEDURES

Equipment has not changed radically over the past decade, except for the introduction of microwave and convector ovens. The small changes which have taken place, however, represent evolution rather than massive breakthroughs. It is probable that kitchens will not benefit greatly from new technology in the near future except for gradual improvement normally expected from any product.

Much has been made of procedures, included in which is a technique called 'system catering', which resembles applied organisation and methods. Various counter systems have been introduced, such as free-flow, etc., which are merely the result of a particular work study exercise. When caterers take the time to use the very simple but effective work study procedures they will be able to produce the optimum layout and procedure for any catering operation they happen to be in. During the next few years it is certain that more interest will be paid to charting techniques, allowing any caterer to produce his own 'catering system'.

This chapter has dealt with a number of topics which have in common the fact that they are not generally accepted by the industry or indeed are relatively unknown to most managements in the industry. One is obviously not in a position to postulate that they will definitely come about. However, they do indicate the changes in attitude which will be experienced by the industry's management during the next decade.

23
Management audit

A complaint of many caterers is that although management books can be very informative, they have difficulty in applying the concepts to their own business.

In order to aid the reader's application of the concepts of this book, the following list of questions has been compiled, based upon the book's content—the number preceding each heading refers to the appropriate chapter. The caterer should use the list as a questionnaire applied directly to his own business in the same way as a consultant would review a client's operation.

1 MANAGEMENT

1.1   Is each member of management (including departmental heads) responsible for specific areas of cost; do they know about it?

1.2   Is each member of staff who is held directly responsible for cost levels kept up to date with cost information or management accounts?

1.3   Is the organisation structure of the business logical?

1.4   Does management delegate adequately right down the line? Do various levels of management tend to deal with work which should be delegated?

1.5   Do you and members of your staff know the key result areas of staff members' jobs measured against objectives?

1.6   Does each member of staff have a job specification?

1.7   How do you communicate 'down the line'—verbally, in writing, by the use of forms, or by management meetings? Are the methods of communication effective?

1.8   How do you tackle your problem-solving and decision-making? By a logical process, or by hunch?

1.9   Does your control function show deviations from target performance, or merely historical results?

1.10 Is selection made on 'pair of hands' basis, or upon long-term labour strategy?

1.11 In what way are staff being developed to enable them to undertake further responsibility and authority?

1.12 Have the objectives of the business been established?

    (*a*) Main business objective (meal experience).
    (*b*) Growth objective (expansions of the meal experience or the formulation of further meal experience).
    (*c*) Return on capital (financial feasibility of the meal experience).

2 MARKET RESEARCH

2.1   Do you know the boundaries of the catchment area your business serves and the population of that area?

2.2   Do you know how your competitors affect your business, and if they are better at anything than you are?

2.3   Are you aware of the size of the specific socio-economic group which you are attracting to your operation?

2.4   Is the business located in the most prominent position to exploit the market?

2.5   What is the optimum turnover of the establishment based on market research, and has it been achieved?

3 THE 'MEAL EXPERIENCE'

3.1   Have you defined the type of meal experience you are providing and listed its unique selling points?

3.2   Should the operation be providing a novel or 'gimmick' experience, has the market life of the operation been considered and is the capital cost of the gimmick likely to return within its market life?

3.3   Has the main business objective (meal experience) been quantified?

3.4 From the meal experience, has a definite mood been isolated which can be converted into an interior design feature?

3.5 Has the design been governed by detailed budgets?

3.6 Have you compared the marketing requirements listed on page 38 against your business design in marketing terms?

4 PLANNING THE MENU

4.1 What market need does the menu satisfy?

4.2 Does the menu form part of the total meal experience?

4.3 How extensive is the menu?

4.4 What gross margin could be achieved?

4.5 How many dishes result in waste?

4.6 Is the menu well balanced?

4.7 Is the menu imaginative?

4.8 Are the dishes well prepared and presented?

5 MENU MARKETING

5.1 What would a professional opinion of your menu format and copy be likely to be?

5.2 Can the menu be easily read, and a selection made within a few minutes?

5.3 Is the type face or lettering style clear, particularly in a dimly lit room?

5.4 Does the menu contain other promotional information apart from the names of the dishes?

5.5 Does the menu change frequently?

5.6 Are dish prices compatible to quality or produce and market?

5.7 Can the menu generate the target gross profit required?

5.8 Does the overall menu design harmonise with the concept of the establishment?

5.9 Do you analyse dishes sold?

5.10 Do you examine 'average check' trends?

6 THE BACK DOOR

6.1 What procedures are there to ensure that specific goods ordered are actually delivered?

6.2   What procedures are there to ensure that the correct quantity of goods are delivered and charged to the establishment?

6.3   Are all goods weighed on delivery?

6.4   Are specifications of all goods purchased made prior to ordering?

6.5   Is a record kept of all goods inward?

7 REQUISITIONS

7.1   Are requisitions made on special, consecutively numbered forms, signed by both issuer and receiver both of whom have a copy? Is each separate item noted specifically in terms of brand name, weight and size?

7.2   What advantages/disadvantages are likely to accrue if an imprest requisitioning system is utilised in your establishment?

9 CENTRALISATION

*(For caterers with 10 or more units turning over
£1 000 000 per annum in food sales)*

9.1   What research has been carried out into centralisation?

9.2   Have you centralised any products into one unit for the group as a trial, e.g. peeled potatoes, meat pies, soup, etc.?

9.3   Has a feasibility study been carried out to ensure that savings will accrue from centralisation?

9.4   Have the more complex administrative procedures required by the commissary been adequately considered?

10 ADVERTISING AND PROMOTION

10.1   Does your advertising form part of an overall promotional campaign?

10.2   Is the advertising effort considered in terms of:

(*a*)   Timing.
(*b*)   The customer.
(*c*)   Design.

10.3   Is the advertising strategy planned carefully in advance or is it *ad hoc*?

10.4   Are advertising budgets compared with past and likely future results?

10.5   Have all the media available been considered?

10.6   Does your advertising campaign build confidence in the minds of potential customers?

10.7   Have you considered representation as a sales technique?

11 WINE AND LIQUOR PURCHASING

11.1   What overall theme guides the purchase of beverages?

11.2   Does the quality of the wine list match the quality and price of the menu?

11.3   Are all the wines purchased sampled prior to initial delivery?

11.4   What arrangements are available in terms of stock finance?

12 BAR AND CELLAR STOCKHOLDING

12.1   Do you keep stockholdings down to a fixed relation to cost of sales?

12.2   Is stock rotated on a first in, first out basis (FIFO)?

12.3   By what formula is the cash value of stock held in bar and cellar governed?

12.4   Does each bar hold a known 'par stock' maintained by bottle-for-bottle issues?

12.5   Are all bottles marked, except beers and minerals?

12.6   Do bar and cellar records provide an adequate control of stock purchased, delivered or sold?

13 ECONOMICS

13.1   What procedures are in being to manage:

(*a*) The cash flow.
(*b*) The profitability of the business?

13.2   What measures are taken to reduce stockholdings to the lowest possible levels?

13.3   What measures are taken to reduce debtors to the lowest possible levels?

13.4   Do you expect to trade on your creditors, i.e. use outstanding suppliers' accounts as credit, therefore working capital?

13.5   How does your balance sheet stand up to the interpretation of balance sheet ratios?

13.6   Have cost and profit levels been set at a level allowing a reasonable return on capital of the operation?

13.7   What percentage of turnover is administration costs? Is it adequate?

13.8   Do you use a recognised form of catering accounts, e.g. standard hotel accounts?

13.9   Are you aware of the break-even point of your operation?

13.10   What investment criteria do you use for new operations?

14 KITCHEN PLANNING

14.1   Is the kitchen sited in the best possible position compatible with the needs of public areas?

14.2   Has the siting of the kitchen taken into account:

(a) Deliveries.
(b) Service.
(c) Electricity, cables, gas and water pipes.
(d) Sewerage.
(e) Aspect of larder and stores?

14.3   What consideration has been given to walls, floors and ceiling and ventilation?

14.4   What consideration has been given to lighting?

14.5   What consideration has been given to heating and insulation properties of equipment?

14.6   Is space adequate or inadequate for preparation, storage and service?

14.7   Is equipment laid out to afford the greatest economy of movement and effectiveness of storage, preparation and service?

14.8   Is the equipment designed for easy working and cleaning and to prevent accidents?

14.9   Do you use any charting techniques to plan the best equipment layout?

15 PERSONNEL

15.1   What policies are in being to ensure that staff feel secure?

15.2   How do you assess wages payable for a particular job?

15.3   What opportunities exist for promotion?

15.4   Of what standard is staff feeding and accommodation?

15.5   How many people have been promoted in the last six months?

15.6   On what basis are decisions concerning grievances made?

15.7   Is every member of staff aware of his or her importance in the work team?

15.8   How much information concerning the establishment's performance and future plans is made available to the staff?

15.9   Are staff interested in the work they do, and anxious to become skilled?

15.10   Are staff aware of the establishment's place *vis-à-vis* competition?

15.11   Is there a properly organised suggestion scheme?

15.12   Do management and staff meet regularly?

15.13   What perquisites are available to employees?

16 CONTROL

16.1   Is every item of expense made the direct responsibility of specific personnel?

16.2   Is a control factor measured against each item of expense?

16.3   Are measures taken to ensure that common wages frauds do not occur?

16.4   Is the movement of cash and goods monitored by control records through every department?

16.5   Is the control information relevant to the size of the operation?

16.6   Does the control information reveal the data which management needs to take action?

17 FOOD CONTROL

17.1   Does the food-control system monitor the movement of food from the order of raw materials to the customer's plate?

17.2   What costing and sales analysis records are kept to ensure that menus are continuously capable of achieving the target gross margin?

17.3   Are all dishes prepared, specified or written records?

17.4 Can the service of *every item* from kitchen or stillroom be accounted for?

17.5 Can the variances of actual gross profit from target gross profit be identified for decision-making?

18 LIQUOR CONTROL

18.1 Is every item of liquor controlled from delivery, cellar and bar?

18.2 Are stocks taken regularly?

18.3 Are par stocks, bottle-for-bottle requisites and marked bottles incorporated into the system?

19 MANPOWER CONTROL

19.1 What is the labour turnover of the establishment?

19.2 What are the percentages of turnover of the departmental payrolls?

19.3 Do you consider the standard cost of each job?

21 TRAINING

21.1 What is management's view of training?

21.2 Are the staff employed by the establishment fully competent at their craft?

21.3 Are both management and staff aware of the importance of social skills in customer–guest relationships?

21.4 What is management's view of development?

Bibliography

Those food and beverage managers who wish to study the subjects discussed in this book in further depth, or consider alternative points of view, will find the following books of interest in addition to all hotel and catering EDC publications.

ARNHEIM, R. A., *Art and Visual Perception*, Faber, London (1956)

BARTON, A., *The Hungry Executive*, Business Books, London (1972)

BOWER, M., *The Will to Manage*, McGraw–Hill, London (1966)

CAMPBELL-SMITH, G., *The Marketing of the Meal Experience*, The University of Surrey, Guildford

DRUCKER, P., *Managing for Results*, Pan Books, London (1958); *The Practice of Management*, Pan Books, London (1955)

DRUMMOND, J. C. and WILBRAHAM, A., *The Englishman's Food*, Jonathan Cape, London (1957)

FEARN, D. A., *The Practice of General Management: An Hotel and Catering Application*, Macdonald Press, London (1971); available in hard cover as *Management Systems for the Hotel, Catering and Allied Industries*, Business Books, London (1969)

GAGE, W. A., *Value Analysis*, McGraw–Hill, London (1967)

KEPNER, C. and TREGOE, B., *The Rational Manager*, McGraw–Hill, London (1962)

LOCKYER, K., *Critical Path Analysis*, Pitman, London (1964)

ODIORNE, G. S., *Management by Objectives*, McGraw–Hill, London (1966)

RIETZ, C. A., *A Guide to the Selection, Combination and Cooking of Foods*, Avi (1961)

TACK, A., *1000 Ways to Increase Your Sales*, The World's Work (1913) Ltd., London (1954)

WARREN, G. C. (Ed.), *The Foods We Eat*, Cassell, London (1958)

WRIGHT, M. C., *Discounted Cash Flow*, McGraw–Hill, London (1967)

Index